P9-DZX-810

Sunset

TRELLISES
AND ARBORS

BY SCOTT ATKINSON, PHILIP EDINGER
AND THE EDITORS OF SUNSET BOOKS

SUNSET BOOKS · MENLO PARK, CALIFORNIA

SECOND-STORY GARDENING

Reach new heights in landscape design with a trellis or arbor as your springboard. These upwardly mobile structures do more than provide shade, shelter, and privacy: they stretch garden space, giving you more growing area as well as a host of vertical design possibilities. Trellises and arbors can serve as both focal points or backdrops; they can reconfigure the landscape by providing transitions that hide the areas beyond from direct view. Use them to link garden areas into a series of separate outdoor realms; or let them join spaces via a repeating trellis design, a long pergola, or an extensive overhead.

Vertical gardening isn't new, but it's being rediscovered with new enthusiasm. Some trellises and arbors are classics, while others are more playful. You can make them as simple or as fancy as you choose. Given the surge in interest, you'll find no lack of designs to buy or build.

This book works both sides of the fence. If you're just browsing for ideas, see the photos in Chapter 1, "Going Vertical," a visual survey of trellis and arbor options. If it's plants you're after, you'll find them in Chapter 2, "A Collection of Climbers." Chapters 3 and 4—"Trellis Projects" and "Arbor Ideas"— are for builders looking for do-it-yourself inspiration. Do you have questions about lumber, tools, and building techniques? Turn to Chapter 5, "Nuts and Bolts."

Use this book to design and build an arbor or trellis, then adorn it with plants—or just take a detour to wherever your interests lie.

SUNSET BOOKS

Vice President, Sales: Richard A. Smeby
Editorial Director: Bob Doyle
Production Director: Lory Day
Art Director: Vasken Guiragossian

Staff for this book:

Managing Editor: Suzanne Normand Eyre
Copy Editor and Indexer: Rebecca LaBrum
Photo Researcher: Tishana Peebles
Production Coordinator: Patricia S. Williams
Special Contributors: Lisa Anderson, Jean Warboy

Art Director: Alice Rogers
Principal Illustrator: Mark Pechenik,
Additional Illustrations: Catherine M. Watters
Computer Production: Fog Press

Cover: Photography by Derek Fell. Border photograph by Jerry Pavia.

DESIGN CREDITS

Ralph Barnes: 7 bottom right; **John M. Bernhard:** 81 bottom; **Tom Chakas:** 7 bottom center, 21 bottom right; **Bill Derringer & Associates:** 13 bottom, 84; **Eichengreen Design:** 27 bottom right; **Kent Gordon England:** 6 top right; **Jeffrey B. Glander & Associates:** 4; **John Herbst:** 79; **Patrick J. Killen:** 11 top left; **Jim Long:** 15 bottom left; **Evani Lupinek:** 66 top; **Matterhorn Nursery:** 9 top right; **Occidental Arts & Ecology:** 9 bottom left; **Gary Orr:** 12 top right; **Mark Pechenik:** 92 top; **Cassie Picha Design:** 9 middle right, 26 top; **Joleen and Tony Morales of Redwood Landscape:** 9 bottom right; **David Reed:** 87 top left; **Susan Schieson Design:** 16; **Michael Schultz Design:** 24 top; **Margaret de Haas Van Dorsser:** 14 top right; **Waterman & Sun:** 88 top; **Ted Wells:** 11 top right; **Richard William:** 71 top right; **Kenneth W. Wood:** 89 middle; **Phil Wood:** 7 top right.

First printing January 1999

Copyright © 1999 Sunset Publishing Corporation, Menlo Park, CA 94025. First edition. All rights reserved, including the right of reproduction in whole or in part in any form. Library of Congress Catalog Card Number: 98-86303. ISBN 0-376-03782-2.

Printed in the United States.

PHOTOGRAPHERS

William D. Adams: 42 bottom left; **Scott Atkinson:** 106; **Dale Berman:** 11 top left; **Marion Brenner:** 7 bottom right, 9 bottom left; **David Cavagnaro:** 38 bottom left, 43 bottom left; **Peter Christiansen:** 64 left, 64 top right , 64 bottom right, 65 left; **Glenn Cormier:** 11 top right, 93 top; **Crandall & Crandall:** 7 bottom left; **Mark Darley:** 8 top left; **R. Todd Davis:** 39 top right, 41 bottom left, 43 bottom right, 46 right, 49 left, back cover top right; **William B. Dewey:** 32 top, 93 bottom; **John R. Dunmire:** 44 bottom right; **Derek Fell:** 17 top right, 19 top left, 30 left, 36 left, 39 bottom, 41 top right, 48 bottom left, 51 middle, 73 middle; **Anne Garrison:** 22 top; **Jay Graham:** 12 top right; **Lynne Harrison:** 3 middle left, 6 bottom left, 6 bottom right, 7 top right, 9 middle right, 10 top left, 13 top left, 15 top left, 15 bottom right, 16, 17 bottom left, 18 left, 19 top right, 24 top, 26 top, 27 bottom left, 27 bottom right, 34 bottom right, 45 middle right, 52 top, 54, 87 top; **Philip Harvey:** 23, 27 top left, 96, 98 left, 103 bottom, 107 all; **Saxon Holt:** 3 middle right, 10 bottom right, 19 bottom, 25 top left, 31 top right, 31 bottom, 33 middle, 34 middle, 39 top left, 45 bottom right, 46 top left, 53 right, 73 left, 74, 78; **Dency Kane:** 3 top right, 7 top middle, 9 top right, 28 all; **Randy Leffingwell:** 20 top right; **David Duncan Livingston:** 21 top; **Allan Mandell:** 3 top left, 4 all, 7 bottom middle, 8 top middle, 8 top right, 8 bottom right, 10 bottom left, 14 top right, 20 bottom left, 21 bottom right; **Charles Mann:** 7 top left, 12 middle left, 14 bottom right, 15 bottom left, 17 top left, 36 bottom right, 37 bottom left, 37 bottom right, 48 top left, 50 bottom left; **David McDonald:** 7 middle left, 8 bottom left, 33 bottom, 38 right, 47 left; **Jerry Pavia:** 15 top right, 37 top right, 38 top left, 39 middle, 40 right, 40 bottom left, 47 top right, 49 right, 50 top left, 50 middle left, 50 middle right, 51 top, 51 bottom right, 53 left; **Norman A. Plate:** 3 bottom, 6 top right, 7 middle right, 13 bottom, 31 top left, 57 all, 63 top, 65 top right, 79 all, 94, 97, 98 right, 99 top left, 99 bottom, 100, 101, 102, 103 top, 104 all, 105 all, back cover top left; **Rob Proctor:** 18 bottom right, 20 top left; **John Rizzo:** 15 middle left; **Susan A. Roth:** 6 top left, 22 bottom, 34 top right, 41 bottom right, 42 middle left, 43 top left, 44 top left, 85, back cover bottom left; **Richard Shiell:** 36 top right; **Michael Skott:** 14 top left, 14 bottom left; **Joseph B. Strauch, Jr.:** 35 bottom, 42 bottom right; **Sean Sullivan:** 65 bottom right; **K. Bryan Swezey:** 26 bottom; **Michael S. Thompson:** 9 top left, 24 bottom, 27 top right, 30 top right, 35 left, 35 top right, 37 top left, 40 top left, 43 middle right, 43 top right, 45 top left, 45 top right, 45 bottom left, 47 bottom left, 48 top right; **Don Vandervort:** 1 all, 17 bottom right, 25 bottom, 32 bottom, 52 bottom; **Peter O. Whiteley:** 9 bottom right, 11 bottom right, 12 top left, 12 bottom left, 13 top right, 21 bottom left, 83; **Bob Wigand:** 18 top right; **Doug Wilson:** 63 bottom; **Martha Woodward:** 33 top; **Tom Woodward:** 34 left, 42 top left, 43 middle, 44 bottom left, 46 bottom left, 51 bottom, 53 bottom; **Tom Wyatt:** 25 top right, 88, 89.

For additional copies of *Trellises and Arbors* or any other *Sunset* book, call 1-800-526-5111.

CONTENTS

GOING VERTICAL

Running out of garden space? Need to frame a favorite view or hide the neighbors' peeling paint? Want to link disparate landscape elements, direct foot traffic, or define an outdoor retreat or entertaining area?

Think trellises and arbors. Ranging from traditional to trendy to quirky, these familiar frames offer firm footholds for vines and vegetables while stretching garden space skyward. You'll discover a whole new world of vertical expressions: structures that are focal points, backdrops that add depth and layering, designs that shape a view and those that provide shade, screening, and style.

This first chapter is intended as a visual introduction to the art of choosing and using arbors and trellises. Scores of colorful photos show you classic gridwork frames, entry arches, patio roofs, pergolas, and gazebos; you'll see rustic twig and bamboo structures as well as those made from found objects (old chairs and headboards, for example!). Look here for inspiration—one or more of these ideas may be just right for your garden.

Most arbors carry vines, but this two-post design holds up a hammock, too.

ENTER THE TRELLIS

Whether it flanks a patio door, props up a riot of roses, cages tomatoes or pole beans, or livens up a large, boring lawn, a trellis can bring a touch of the Rockies to an otherwise Kansas-like vista. Walls and fences perform this function, too, but trellises do it with a superbly open feel—and the resulting dappled sunlight, breezes, and patches of blue sky counter any potential "prison-wall" effect.

The trellis ranges from humble to grand, utilitarian to sculptural; you can opt for a gridlike, symmetrical style or a more whimsical, gnarled look. What's important is that the trellis fits in with the rest of the garden and easily shoulders the weight of the plants you choose for it. A lightweight trellis might back a modest container plant; a large, sturdy frame can dress up a garage wall or form a backdrop for an entire garden.

THIS PAGE, CLOCKWISE FROM TOP RIGHT: An arch-topped patio trellis made from birch twigs; a white-painted lattice screen with oval-framed "window"; an open and airy lath fence; a freestanding pillar that's smothered in roses.

OPPOSITE PAGE, CLOCKWISE FROM TOP LEFT: A rough and rustic lathwork fan; a decorative garden obelisk; an ornate fencetop trellis with hanging plants below; a surfaced-cedar planter box backdrop; whimsically whorled reinforcing-bar sculpture; a corner "climber" trellis, also shaped from reinforcing bar; a shed-obscuring lathwork wall; rose-supporting rooftop rungs.

INTRODUCING ARBORS

Arbors take things one step further, adding a third dimension to the trellis's upward leap. In its simplest form, an arbor takes parallel trellis walls and adds a third trellis as a roof.

Classic "arch arbors" curve the roof. Spread things out and add built-in benches (and perhaps a trickling wall fountain), and you have a bower—a quiet retreat for reading or moon-watching. A heavier, longer arbor laid out colonnade fashion becomes a pergola; it's traditionally shored up with stout timber posts, poles, or cast masonry columns. An arbor on a larger scale, with uniform dimension lumber or wrought-iron framing, becomes an architectural overhead and serves as an extension of interior living space. And if you take a remote, freestanding arbor and give it six or eight sides, lattice walls, and toeholds for plants, you'll have a gazebo.

CLOCKWISE FROM TOP LEFT: An arbor with sides made from a salvaged orchard ladder, bridged with 2 by 4 beams; a tunnel arbor with wide trellis walls, buried in cottage-garden color; wire plant supports climbing a pergola's columns; a flat-top bower with built-in bench; a two-post door frame leading to a lush garden beyond.

CLOCKWISE FROM TOP LEFT: A formal painted arbor with eyebrow roof and gridwork trellis wings; a rustic twig arch that spans a pathway; copper hoops with twiglike styling; a wavy arbor with posts and beams saw-shaped from standard lumber; a "living arbor" twined together to form support for other plants.

WHERE DO THEY GO?

Trellises—and often arbors, too—can go just about anywhere you like. For starters, explore these options.

Front gate. An arched entry arbor, perhaps joined by a matching gate and white picket fence, offers a traditional welcoming touch. Or choose a more rustic, flat-roofed structure. Just be sure it's at least 7 feet tall and 5 feet wide for easy traffic flow.

Front porch. An eyebrow arbor spreads a bright patch of bougainvillea or wisteria atop the front door. Flanking trellises allow climbing roses a foothold up and over.

Entry courtyard. If you're looking for extra living space, why not reclaim the front yard? Line garden walls with trellised plants; an overhead provides shade in summer and shelter in winter.

Sideyards. Lead the way with an arch arbor; line house walls and border fences with trellises stretching towards the sun.

CLOCKWISE FROM TOP LEFT: A casual flat-topped entry arbor frames a flagstone path leading to the front door; a formal white arch marks a winding path and is flanked by crisp lattice walls; a country cottage door is shaded by wire-trained plantings.

CLOCKWISE FROM LEFT: A U-shaped courtyard is bridged by a formal, concrete columned pergola; a bright red door—a frame within a frame—leads from one garden zone to another; a stucco-columned overhead ties together garage and guest cottage while housing built-in benches, garden furniture, and even a hot tub.

Patios and decks. Backyard hardscapes are naturals for arbors and trellises. Lath or wire trellises mask house walls in greenery or serve as backdrops for colorful container plantings. An overhead turns the space into a shady outdoor room, perhaps providing privacy from neighbors. A swimming pool's borders might be marked by a poolside bower (but watch those falling leaves).

Fences and garden walls. Masonry walls are ready-made backdrops for espalier and wire-supported plantings. Wood house siding and wood fences can double as trellises with wire, lath, or lattice; just be sure to float the supports a few inches off the wood to allow air space and room for plants to grow (see page 72 for pointers). A fence becomes open and airy with the addition of a trellis up top (see page 73). Hang planter boxes off the inside edge or add crosspieces for hanging containers.

Vegetable gardens. A-frames hold beans, peas, and melons above the vegetable garden plains. Flat trellises can back up raised planting beds, mark space, and provide a decorative backdrop while doubling your growing area.

Open spaces. A broad expanse of lawn or a wide planting bed calls for a freestanding trellis or arbor to showcase a prized vine or provide a vertical contrast to lower-growing plants. An arch arbor—built from wire, pipe, or limber wooden boughs—frames a view; a casual garden path winds through and beyond.

Remote corners. If your landscape warrants it, why not make a private retreat with a bower or gazebo festooned with lush vines? A shady pergola can lead the way.

THIS PAGE, CLOCKWISE FROM TOP LEFT: Three sizes of pressure-treated poles bear the weight of heavy vines and screen out neighbors; overhead space frames support vines and bench swing while defining a series of outdoor "rooms"; a sideyard fence is relieved by notched-in pockets and airy latticework; a wood-and-wire alcove forms a garden focal point.

OPPOSITE PAGE, CLOCKWISE FROM TOP LEFT: A gridwork trellis turns a potentially boring wall into leafy art; an aging fence gets a facelift— and some needed reinforcement—via strong, soaring arbors and screens; twin storage sheds are wrapped in trellises and hold up a shady lattice roof.

THIS PAGE, CLOCKWISE FROM TOP LEFT: A single pyracantha is trained espalier-style atop a spacer-mounted grid of cedar 1 by 2s; simple, ladderlike walls and roof form a doorway through raised planting beds; bentwood twig arches add a rustic touch to a transition zone; a neighborly fence leaves plenty of open areas along its series of linked, trellis-lined sections.

OPPOSITE PAGE, CLOCKWISE FROM TOP LEFT: Trellis towers back up a vegetable garden's orderly rows; bamboo tepees and cross-rungs stand up to sprawling pole beans; a bamboo-and-twine container cage adds a sculptural flourish; rustic twigs are artfully joined in a twist on the classic gazebo; a lat-ticework trellis backs up a raised planter box and doubles as a space-dividing screen.

WHAT'S YOUR STYLE?

Your trellis or arbor should harmonize with both house and garden. The trellis may be smothered in plants most of the year, but come season's end, it's the structure—not the plants—that will take center stage. In basic terms, garden styles can be divided into formal and casual schools. Formal styles feature rectilinear lines and crisp corners; casual landscapes make use of looser, more rustic shapes.

Traditional homes and gardens, on the formal plan, are echoed by clean-lined wood lath and lumber; rustic or cottage-garden schemes might use quirky, freeform materials and found objects. A romantic garden can be dressed in gingerbread lattice and accessorized with curved Victorian trim; a modernistic landscape calls for spare, clean-lined wood and steel or sweeping, sculptural shapes. Eclectic gardens may have whimsical period blends or stark, postmodern, sculpted-looking pieces. Regional themes abound (a Southwestern style, for instance); these normally include local landscape materials and motifs. But rules are meant to be broken, and sometimes the most creative designs draw from a number of styles.

Your trellis or arbor should match the scale of its surroundings. A large architectural overhead could overpower an intimate backyard space; a trellis that looks dynamic close up might be lost in a wide sweep of lawn.

OPPOSITE PAGE: An evenly spaced grid of traditional painted lath forms a stylish privacy screen and helps turn a peaked overhead into a formal outdoor room.

THIS PAGE, CLOCKWISE FROM TOP LEFT: A wood-and-steel arch arbor looks right at home amidst a spill of cottage-garden plantings; a formal gazebo is a quiet and romantic destination; an L-shaped arbor hangs over a detached seating area; a wall trellis employs a touch of forced perspective to "stretch" a small space.

THIS PAGE, CLOCKWISE FROM ABOVE:
Floral chaos washes around a
recycled blue stool serving as a trellis;
a garden playhouse made from
lashed branches forms a shady spot
for afternoon tea parties; a sculpture
of gnarled branches seems to grow
from amid its surroundings.

OPPOSITE PAGE, CLOCKWISE FROM TOP LEFT:
A dimension-lumber arbor with
angled beams and braces divides one
garden zone from another; welded
steel hoops and crossrungs form an
arching space frame; an open, rustic
overhead combines weathered 6 by 6
posts and beams with a simple roof of
galvanized plumbing pipe.

THIS PAGE, CLOCKWISE FROM TOP LEFT: Twiggy backdrop trellises add playful accents to a stone-ringed vegetable and cutting garden; a fantasy in grass includes an outdoor "bedroom" with recycled headboard trellis and a screen wall made from wire grid and climbing roses; a lathwork trellis grows bird-houses, not bougainvillea.

OPPOSITE PAGE, CLOCKWISE FROM TOP: A wisteria-bearing bamboo trellis screens a delightfully disparate garden; a "planted" trellis of bent reinforcing bar grows up a stucco house wall; 8-foot-tall metal globe trellises, festooned with wisteria, can be illuminated at night by glowing blue uplights.

ADDING AMENITIES

Extras can turn an arbor or trellis into something really special. Trellises benefit from some accent flourishes; arbor options help transform the basic structure into an outdoor room fit for active entertaining or quiet relaxation. Here's a list to consider.

Screens. An arbor or trellis may be flanked by wooden or metal screens to make "walls"—adding a sense of enclosure, providing a windbreak, and offering vertical support for climbing vines.

Roofing. Place a roof atop overhead arbor supports and turn a simple structure into an outdoor room shielded from the elements. Open roofing—wood slats, for example—leaves gaps, allowing some sunlight, breezes, and moisture to pass through. Solid roofing materials—such as shingles, shakes, fiberglass, or steel—keep out the elements. If you're thinking of a solid roof, be sure to slope it for runoff and, if necessary, beef it up to carry the weight of snow.

Built-in furniture. The posts or walls of an arbor or pergola may provide a good anchor for built-in wooden benches, traditional features in bowers and gazebos. A bench can even be backed with a simple trellis. Raise the "bench," and it becomes a table or serving counter. For summertime leisure, you might include a hanging swing or hammock.

Planter boxes. Much like benches, raised boxes can front a trellis or mark out the space below an arbor. Container "clusters" also define and stretch growing space, direct traffic, and create a pleasant, cottage-garden clutter. And what about letting containers hang from arbor beams or rafters or from a simple crosspiece that turns your two-dimensional trellis into a three-dimensional arbor?

Drip tubing. It's usually a simple matter to snake drip tubing and fittings through trellis and arbor supports, providing easy-care watering for your vines. (For added convenience, consider hooking the system to an automatic timer.) Roof-mounted spray emitters provide a cooling mist on hot summer days—pleasing to both plants and people.

Water features. While we're on the subject of water, keep in mind that the outdoor room formed by your arbor or trellis is perfectly complemented by the soothing sights and sounds of a wall fountain, tub garden, or small pond. To recycle water for a spill fountain, spray fountain, or formal wall fountain, you'll need some tubing, a fountain jet, and a small recirculating pump. Some home supply centers and mail-order sources combine these components in kit form.

Light fixtures. Why not showcase an arbor or trellis at night while providing general light for paths and garden seating? Low-voltage fixtures are easy to install and safest to operate, but line-voltage (120-volt) fixtures offer extra punch.

A little light goes a long way at night. Discreet downlights can be anchored to posts and overhead beams; uplights wash plants from below. Path lights lead the way. And what about a string of low-voltage incandescent strip lights to outline the structure and add a touch of fun?

BELOW: A little night light highlights plantings and helps turn an architectural overhead into an around-the-clock extension of interior space. Discreet downlights provide ambient and accent light; strip lights along horizontal beams are almost purely for fun.

OPPOSITE PAGE, TOP: An inviting private courtyard includes an arching architectural overhead above the correspondingly arched entry. The space enjoys morning sunlight, but thanks to the fireplace, it's also used for evening entertaining.

OPPOSITE PAGE, BOTTOM: A simple, square structure forms an entry arch that's roofed and walled with climbing roses; built-in benches help brace the arbor's posts.

THIS PAGE, TOP: A formal outdoor room is furnished with a stone-lined bench, a small pond, and a collection of container plants. An elephant head forms the playful wall fountain.

THIS PAGE, AT RIGHT: A lattice-lined bower has the traditional gambrel-shaped roof above and built-in bench seating below, forming a quiet, shady retreat for reading, snacking, or doing absolutely nothing.

OPPOSITE PAGE, CLOCKWISE FROM TOP LEFT: A shady rose arbor doubles as the frame for a bench swing; an architectural overhead has closely spaced lath roofing and a network of misters to keep both plants and people cool; a steel-frame backyard ramada houses a barbecue and dining area.

GETTING STARTED

Ready to get in gear? First, decide on a spot and a function. Will your arbor or trellis be a focal point or a backdrop, a garden star or an unsung workhorse? How much weight must the structure support? How much sunlight, shade, and wind does the site receive? Think style, too, and consider amenities like fountains, benches, containers for plants, and lighting. Determine whether you'll build or buy.

If you intend to buy your arbor or trellis, see pages 64–65 for shopping tips. You can also enlist the aid of a landscape professional or build the structure yourself, using Chapters 3 and 4—"Trellis Projects" and "Arbor Ideas" —for inspiration. Most of our projects require only basic building skills, such as measuring, sawing, and fastening; for the fine points, see Chapter 5, "Nuts and Bolts."

When you're ready for the finishing touch—the plants— simply turn the page.

THIS PAGE, TOP: A highly crafted maze of twigs and branches adds up to an arched outdoor room, forming a stylish focal point while shading a rustic garden bench.

THIS PAGE, AT LEFT: A fruiting arbor bears grapefruit and tangelos. These 14-year-old plants are standard (not dwarf) trees; they reached the overhead in 2 years. Careful pruning and training makes them conform to the arbor.

OPPOSITE PAGE, CLOCKWISE FROM TOP LEFT: A gravel path curves through a rustic, ladderlike arbor lushly laden with plants; containers sprout loopy supports styled from flexible copper tubing; copper supply pipe and fittings form a freestanding, pyramidal pillar; colorful orcas ride high above a spare supporting frame below.

The unadorned trellis or arbor is an unfinished work of art: only when you add a vine do you complete the piece. But which vine will provide that perfect complement?

A COLLECTION OF
CLIMBERS

The following pages offer you plenty of choices. You'll find vines of all sizes and for all climates,

kinds that retain foliage all year and sorts that shed their leaves each fall, vines that are striking from afar and others that instead reward close-up inspection. Some have foliage so dense it makes a living wall of green, while others form merely a delicate tracery of stems and foliage. Most have flowers—and among these, many are fragrant. A few even bear tasty fruit.

Turn the page—and begin your search for the finishing touch that will make your trellis or arbor beautifully complete.

Ever-popular wisteria offers an arresting combination of rugged strength and ethereal beauty.

CHOOSING THE RIGHT VINE

How do you achieve the ideal adornment for your trellis, arbor, or pergola? The process starts with selecting a plant that can successfully climb the support and that suits it in general scale. Once that's done, you'll need to plant the vine properly and attend to some routine maintenance as it grows—training, pruning, and thinning.

An ironwork fence is a congenial host to a large-flowered hybrid clematis.

HOW VINES CLIMB

You can't expect a vine to obediently climb any support you give it. Though some can manage the task, most will simply sprawl or tangle for lack of anything to hang onto. To know what sort of structure a vine can scale, you need to know just how that plant climbs.

Lonicera × heckrottii twining on lattice

TWINING VINES. Vines such as honeysuckle (*Lonicera*, page 45), send out stems that coil around anything slender, growing upward in the process. In nature, they often wrap around the branches of other plants, which then in effect become living trellises. For upward growth, twiners need wire, string, or doweling.

COILING TENDRILS AND LEAFSTALKS. Vines such as grape (*Vitis*, page 52) and sweet pea (*Lathyrus odoratus*, page 43) climb by means of specialized growths that reach out and wrap around anything handy. Usually forked or branched, these tendrils arise directly from the stem or, in some individuals, form a part of the leaves. In some vines, such as cat's claw (*Macfadyena unguis-cati*, page 46), the tendrils can hook into rough surfaces. A few vines (clematis, page 37, is the most familiar) have leafstalks that behave like tendrils, coiling around any slender support they encounter.

Like twining vines, those that climb by tendrils and coiling leafstalks need fairly slender vertical supports: wire, rope, dowels or rods, or narrow lath.

VINE ATTACHMENTS

Twining stems

Tendrils

Holdfast discs

Aerial rootlets

No means of attachment

CLINGING STEMS. Specialized stem growths such as holdfast (suction) discs and aerial rootlets firmly attach stems of these vines to all but slick surfaces. In general, clinging vines are poor candidates for trellises and arbors: you can't easily guide their growth (they attach wherever they want to), thinning and pruning involve physically detaching them from their support, and growth is typically so dense it obscures the support. Ivy *(Hedera)* is a well-known example.

CLAMBERING VINES. These plants produce long, flexible stems that have no means of attachment, though some have thorns that help them hook their way through other plants. All such vines must be tied to their supports. Climbing roses (page 49) and bougainvillea (page 37) are two familiar clambering vines.

ABOVE: Latticework provides perfect support for climbing roses; canes can be tied to members or woven through openings.

BELOW: A series of strategically placed wisterias transforms an ambitious arbor into a cool, fragrant tunnel of blossoms and leaves.

Robust *Jasminum polyanthum* engulfs a sturdy pergola in a scented cloud of white blossoms.

MATCHING VINE TO SUPPORT

Which comes first, the plant or the trellis? It can work both ways. Sometimes you fall in love with a particular vine, then choose the structure that best suits it. Just as often, though, you already have a completed support structure and need to select a vine to decorate it. In either case, it's important to achieve a compatible union between plant and support. The following discussion assumes you have

ABOVE: Luxuriant bougainvillea needs sturdy support for its prolonged fanfare of neon-bright color.

RIGHT: Fire-engine red arbor and golden-leafed hop vine (*Humulus lupulus* 'Aureus') are an electrifying duet.

the support and now need to choose a vine. If the reverse is true, the advice still applies—but in reverse!

Begin with the obvious. If you have a large support—an arbor or pergola, for example—pick a large-growing vine that will give you the coverage you want. Likewise, if you have only a modest trellis, steer clear of the vining Godzillas. Once you've decided on the proper plant size, consider what sort of climber the support can handle best. Does it provide footholds for tendrils or twining, or would those sorts of vines need additional encouragement? If so, how easily can you provide it?

Now narrow your selection to vines that will succeed in your area. Consult the zone descriptions and map on pages 108–111 to find your *Sunset* climate zone; when you look through the vine descriptions on pages 34–53, consider only plants recommended for your zone.

PLANTING AND TRAINING

Most vines are sold in nursery containers that range in size from 4-inch pots to 1-, 2-, and 5-gallon cans. Though you can buy the plants at any time of year when soil is not frozen, there are preferred planting times. Where winters are relatively mild, it's best to

plant during winter; this gives roots plenty of time to establish before warm weather sets in and the growing season begins. In cold-winter regions, plant as early as you can in spring to give vines as long a cool-weather establishment period as possible.

You can also plant in spring and summer, of course—but plants set out in warmer weather must cope with heat stress (rapid transpiration that can lead to wilting) while simultaneously trying to establish themselves in your garden. And spring- and summer-planted vines usually put on much less growth during their first year than do vines planted in the cooler months.

In the first several years, while a young vine is growing into its support, you'll need to guide its stems toward your desired goals. For vines that twine or grow by tendrils, be sure to provide the necessary slender vertical members. Whenever needed to prevent tangling, untwine or detach stems that wrap around or cling to one another. If you're growing a vine that has no means of attachment, be sure to tie its stems to the trellis or arbor as they lengthen.

Vines of any sort can become heavy as they increase in size. If not securely attached to the support, mature plants may become dislodged by wind, rain, or their own sheer weight. It's a good idea, therefore, to tie even twiners and tendril-climbers at strategic points to the structure holding them aloft.

Eyescrews are invaluable training aids, particularly for clambering vines. Tie stems directly to the "eyes"; or (as shown here) stretch wires between eyescrews and tie growth to the wires.

LEFT: Good pruning starts with good, sharp pruning shears.
BELOW: Dormant vine shows result of careful and fairly heavy pruning and thinning. Twiggy and weak stems have been pruned out; principal and secondary branches have been spaced out and firmly tied to their trellis support.

PRUNING AND THINNING

No set rule will tell you how much pruning a vine will need: the amount necessary depends on the plant's age, health, and inherent vigor, and on where it's growing. A healthy wisteria, for example, sends out miles of new growth streamers in spring and summer. If the plant's support is limited in extent, some of this growth will need to be guided into place, while the rest should be removed (if you turn your back on it, you may find it invading nearby shrubs and trees). If the wisteria is cloaking a large pergola, though, the rampant new growth will have much more space to occupy; in this case, pruning and thinning aren't as much of an issue.

During a vine's formative years, work toward developing a structure of climbing stems. Don't hesitate to remove unnecessary growth that competes with the main structural development or that is heading in unwanted directions and cannot be guided back into place. In later years, most pruning will involve removing dead or weak stems and thinning out excess growth to untangle a plant and/or reveal more of the support structure. (Certain climbing roses are an exception; they need some annual pruning and thinning to look their best.) For detailed pruning information on individual vines, consult *Sunset's Pruning* (1998).

A SELECTION OF VINES

The following 20 pages present pro-files of popular vines to add just the right finishing touch to your arbor, trellis, or pergola. The selections here offer plenty of variety. You'll find plants that love the sun and those that thrive in shade; tough types for snowy territory as well as tender beauties for mild regions; deciduous vines and evergreen sorts; peren-nial choices and even annuals to grow from seed. And many have fabulous flowers, handsome foliage, or colorful (even edible) fruits—or all three.

Akebia quinata

Each entry opens with the plant's botanical name, followed by its common name (if it has one). The next lines specify whether the plant is evergreen or deciduous and note the climate zones (see pages 108–111) in which it suc-ceeds. Every description tells you how the vine climbs and gives details on its foliage, flowers and/or fruit (where applicable), and ultimate size. We also suggest the best uses and appropriate sup-ports for each plant, and address any cultural or maintenance fea-tures critical to its success.

ACTINIDIA

🌿 DECIDUOUS ✂ ZONES VARY BY SPECIES

Two twining vines give you handsome foliage on thick-limbed plants. One species is enjoyed for its rainbow-hued leaves; the other is a green-leafed form famed for its delicious fruits (the kiwi fruit sold commer-cially).

Colorful *A. kolomikta* grows in Zones 2–9, 15–17, 31–41. It's a 15-footer with varie-gated foliage in a sort of abstract-art style: each heart-shaped, 5-inch leaf may be solid green, green splashed with varied amounts of white, or green boldly patterned in rose pink to nearly red. Because cool weather encourages the most vibrant colors and greatest variegation, this species looks its best in cool spring temper-atures and in cool-summer regions; for the best color in warm-summer areas, choose a location in light shade. As is true for kiwi (below), vines of *A. kolomikta* are either male (pollen-bearing) or female (fruiting); nurseries usually sell male plants, since they are reputed to produce more colorful foliage.

Actinidia deliciosa

Kiwi (also known as Chinese gooseberry), *A. deliciosa*, grows in Zones 4–9, 12, 14–24, 29–31. It's larger than *A. kolomikta* (to 30 feet), clothed in broadly oval, 5- to 8-inch leaves that are dark green above, furry white beneath. New growth is covered in reddish fuzz. If fruit production is your goal, you'll need two vines—one male, one female ('Chico' and 'Hayward' have good-quality fruit). If you merely want to display the vine's ropelike limbs and bold leaves, however, either sex will satisfy.

Both actinidias are worth showing off for their foliage and strong texture. Give them sturdy support, since mature vines are heavy. *A. kolomikta* adapts to trellis training and is a good candidate for wall decoration or freestanding screens; it also displays well on modest-size arbors. For *A. deliciosa*, larger arbors and pergolas are ideal supports; the vines can provide both decoration and shade. You also can train them along horizontal trellises to ornament the tops of walls and fences.

Actinidia kolomikta

AKEBIA QUINATA
FIVELEAF AKEBIA
🌿 EVERGREEN TO DECIDUOUS
✂ ZONES 3–24, 29–41

If this twining vine were called "climbing clover," more gardeners might pause to read about it. The name would certainly give an accurate impression of the five-lobed leaves—though at 4 inches across, they're a lot larger than garden-variety clover. Despite an ultimate reach of 30 feet or

Akebia quinata

more, fiveleaf akebia has a fine-textured delicacy that makes it a good choice for mass foliage effect; it provides a cloak of greenery rather than a strong design statement. Nonetheless, the unusual spring flowers and even stranger fruits beg for close-up viewing. Each pendent, vanilla-scented flower cluster includes both male and female blossoms. The female flowers, grouped at the cluster base, consist of three shell-like segments in a subtle chocolate purple color, while the smaller, rosy purple male flowers are carried more toward the cluster tip. A scattering of 4-inch-long fruits may come in summer—purplish, sausagelike, and actually edible.

Given an arbor, a pergola, or even a wire fence to cover, fiveleaf akebia easily rises to the occasion. From overhead, it casts good shade; on a wall or fence, its solid cover makes a fine-textured foil to other plants placed in front of it. It grows equally well in sun or shade. In the mildest parts of its range, it retains some or all of its leaves over winter; in colder areas, it's fully deciduous.

Akebia quinata 'Shirobana'

AMPELOPSIS brevipedunculata
PORCELAIN BERRY

🌿 Deciduous ✿ Zones 2–24, 28–41

This vine's looks virtually advertise its kinship to grape. The broad, dark green leaves are three lobed and nearly hand size, borne on stems that climb by tendrils and become quite thick and heavy with age. To complete the picture, grapelike clusters of pea-size fruits appear in fall, ripening from greenish ivory through lavender to a bright, metallic blue; you'll often see a variety of colors in a single cluster.

Ampelopsis brevipedunculata

Porcelain berry advances with such enthusiasm that the handsome plant can soon reach 20 to 30 feet. On a sturdy arbor or pergola, where its vigor and size can be accommodated, it makes a striking cover that casts dappled shade.

ARISTOLOCHIA macrophylla
DUTCHMAN'S PIPE

🌿 Deciduous ✿ Zones 1–24, 29–43

Given the ample water it needs, this is a truly luxuriant vine that quickly gives you a solid screen of leaves—with some truly odd flowers thrown into the bargain. It's an old-fashioned favorite: in old sepia photographs, you'll often see it covering porches and gazebos in a dense cloak of tropically bold foliage. Twining stems bear glossy dark green, broadly heart- to kidney-shaped leaves that can reach 14 inches long; as the vine climbs (to 20 to 30 feet in one growing season),

Aristolochia macrophylla

FAST-GROWING CLIMBERS

Akebia quinata
Ampelopsis brevipedunculata
Aristolochia macrophylla
Clytostoma callistegioides
Distictis
Humulus lupulus
Lonicera
Macfadyena unguis-cati
Passiflora
Polygonum
Pyrostegia venusta
Rosa
Solandra maxima
Vitis
Wisteria

the leaves overlap like shingles. The early summer blossoms are neither profuse nor highly visible (they're often tucked back into the foliage), but they're worth looking for. Borne on a threadlike stalk is a yellowish green tube that curves upward, then flares out into three brownish purple lobes about an inch across; in profile, the blossom suggests a curved tobacco pipe.

Dutchman's pipe is at its best trained vertically on wooden or wire trellises, where its stems can twist and twine. Use it to decorate walls and fences, as a leafy partition between outdoor living areas, or—as in times past—to screen porches and summerhouses. Locate it where strong winds won't tatter the oversize leaves.

Aristolochia macrophylla

BEAUMONTIA grandiflora
EASTER LILY VINE

🌿 EVERGREEN 🌿 ZONES 12, 13, 16, 17, 21–27

The common name tells the story: if you want flowers with the color, shape, size, and even the scent of Easter lilies, this is your vine! And you get a lot of vine, too. The somewhat twining, thick-stemmed plant can reach 30 feet high and wide, making it a good candidate for display on a really large trellis or for training up and over an arbor or pergola. Foliage is in scale with the plant size: each leaf is a glossy dark green oval up to 9 inches long. Bloom time runs from spring into summer.

To achieve true grandeur, Easter lily vine needs good soil, regular moisture, and a long, warm growing season. It's heavy and requires a sturdy support, and when young, it will need some amount of tying to the support.

Beaumontia grandiflora

VINES WITH FRAGRANT FLOWERS

Beaumontia grandiflora
Distictis
Gelsemium sempervirens
Jasminum
Lonicera
Mandevilla laxa
Rosa
Solanum crispum
Stephanotis floribunda
Trachelospermum jasminoides
Wisteria

BIGNONIA capreolata
CROSSVINE

🌿 EVERGREEN TO SEMIEVERGREEN
🌿 ZONES 4–9, 14–24, 26–33

In regions with summer rainfall, this is nearly a "plant it and forget it" vine. It's supremely easy to grow, and tendrils equipped with holdfast discs let the stems climb to 30 feet or more without assistance. All you do is direct the growth and remove tangled and superfluous stems. Springtime clusters of 2-inch, trumpet-shaped, brownish orange flowers with yellow centers are pleasant looking rather than flashy. For brighter blossoms in apricot orange, try the selection 'Tangerine Beauty'. Each glossy dark green leaf has two oval leaflets to 6 inches long and a branching central tendril. The foliage makes a dense cover when vines are grown in sun, a somewhat open cover in light shade. Foliage turns purplish in cold weather; in the coldest zones, plants lose some leaves in winter.

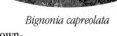

Bignonia capreolata

Given a trellis to cover, crossvine will do the job completely (and attach itself firmly to the support). Large and/or tall arbors are likewise fair game, proving no obstacle to this vine's vigor.

BOUGAINVILLEA

🌿 Evergreen ✿ Zones 12, 13, 15–17, 19, 22–28

A bougainvillea in full, bright bloom evokes images of tropical climes, whitewashed walls, and tiled roofs. In fact, the actual flowers are inconspicuous; it's the bracts (modified leaves) surrounding them that provide those flamboyant, travel-poster hues of purple, magenta, pink, red, orange, yellow, and white. The main bloom period comes in summer, but where winters are mild, vines can flower from spring through fall.

All vining bougainvilleas (there are shrubby types, too) are vigorous and fast growing, reaching 15 to 30 feet depending on the variety. The 2½-inch leaves are heart shaped. The stiff stems are armed with needlelike thorns but have no means of attachment, so you'll need to tie bougainvillea to its support at least during its early years, while it's forming a branch framework. Its uses are varied. Grow it on a trellis to blanket a fence or form a freestanding wall of color; or train it on an arbor, where it soon reaches the top, then spreads out to provide dappled shade beneath its canopy of blossoms.

Essentially frost-free climates are best for bougainvillea, but even in slightly colder zones, established vines will quickly bounce back from the occasional light frost. Where light frosts are common in winter, locate bougainvillea in the garden's warmest spot; an ideal place is against a sheltered, sunny wall (rather than exposed on an arbor).

Bougainvillea 'James Walker'

Bougainvillea on arbor

CLEMATIS

🌿 Deciduous (with one exception) ✿ Zones vary by species

Discerning gardeners have long known the beauties of clematis. Now these aristocratic vines have gone mainstream, available in wide variety from nurseries and garden centers as well as by mail-order. The spectacular large-flowered hybrids have led the charge—they're too pretty to resist, and gardeners who succumb to their allure have learned that clematis culture is not difficult. Species clematis also are entering the general nursery trade in increasing numbers; their individual blossoms may not be as opulent as those of the hybrids, but they make up for any lack of floral size in sheer volume of bloom, charm of flower form, or both.

The chief bloom times are spring and summer. Most clematis flower in one of these two seasons, though some put on a second, smaller display at some point after the first flush has finished. In many clematis, the flowers are followed by silky, subtly decorative seed tassels. (The true flowers of clematis are tiny and inconspicuous; what appear to be showy, colorful petals—and are traditionally referred to as such—are in fact petal-like sepals surrounding the clustered true flowers.)

Large-flowered hybrid clematis mingle effectively on trelliswork of cut bamboo.

Clematis, large-flowered hybrid

Clematis vines are rather thin stemmed and brittle, and young plants in particular need protection from accidental damage. The vines climb by coiling their leafstalks around slender supports such as string, wire, or branches of other plants; any trellis that includes thin members, has a fairly open structure, or incorporates wire will provide good support. Given wire or string to climb, these are superb plants for training on pillars. Only the largest-growing species will make a satisfactory covering for an arbor or pergola. Plants need good soil (the sort you'd give your best vegetables) and regular watering. The ideal planting location puts the top growth in sun, but leaves the soil shaded and cool.

LARGE-FLOWERED HYBRIDS. Despite their varied ancestries, these form a fairly uniform group. Most succeed in Zones 2–9, 14–17, 31–41 and achieve heights of 8 to 15 feet. The usual bloom time is summer. Flowers reach 5 to 10 inches across, with a single row of petals that open out flat and surround a central clump of stamens. Colors include white, lavender, purple, dark to light blue, pink, red, and cream; some types feature a contrasting wash or bar of color down each petal. General nurseries still offer old favorites like sky blue 'Ramona', lilac pink 'Nelly Moser', and even one of the first hybrids—dark purple *C.* × *jackmanii*. But dozens of newer beauties are becoming more widely available. Just choose according to the color you want— they're all lovely!

Clematis 'Perle d'Azur'

SPECIES. No blanket description covers the multitude of clematis species. Some of the most garden-worthy and widely sold choices are described below, presented in order of decreasing cold tolerance.

C. alpina (Zones 1–6, 15–17, 31–43) is a 12-foot vine that flowers in spring, its blossoms dangling at the ends of long stalks. Each 1- to 1½-inch flower has four pointed petals that spread out like a flared skirt. Named varieties offer blooms in white, blue, purple, pink, and red.

C. texensis (Zones 2–9, 14–17, 29–41), called scarlet clematis, is a vine of modest size (to about 10 feet). Unusual lily-shaped, 1-inch red blossoms are carried on upright stems against a backdrop of blue-green leaves; bloom starts in summer and continues into fall. Deep pink 'Duchess of Albany' and dark red 'Lady Bird Johnson' are available varieties.

C. viticella (Zones 2–9, 14–17, 31–41) reaches a vigorous 18 feet and blooms in summer, bearing 2-inch, rosy purple, four-petaled flowers. You'll usually find its named selections and hybrids, such as 'Lady Betty Balfour' (violet), 'Mme. Julia Correvon' (wine red), and 'Polish Spirit' (blue purple).

C. montana (Zones 3–9, 14–17, 31–39), aptly known as anemone clematis, bears blooms with a strong resemblance to Japanese anemones. Vigorous vines to 20 feet or more put on a lavish show in early spring. The basic flower color is white aging to pink, but named varieties offer blooms in pure white and pure pink; *C. m. rubens* has deep pink flowers and bright red new growth that matures to bronzy green.

C. armandii (Zones 4–9, 12–24, 28, 31, warmer parts of 32) is the one evergreen clematis species. In all respects but flower size, it's the giant of the genus. Rapid growth takes it as high as 35 feet; it can easily cloak a large arbor or pergola, where it makes an impressive show. Dark green leaves consist of drooping, narrow, 5-inch leaflets; in early spring, 2½-inch flowers in large, branched clusters engulf the vines in a fragrant white cloud. 'Hendersonii Rubra' is similar to the species but bears pale pink blooms.

TOP: *Clematis montana rubens*
BOTTOM: *Clematis texensis* 'Duchess of Albany'

CLERODENDRUM thomsoniae
BLEEDING HEART GLORYBOWER
🌿 EVERGREEN 🍂 ZONES 22–28

Clerodendrum thomsoniae

In keeping with its tropical origin, bleeding heart glorybower revels in year-round warmth. Given a frost-free garden, the twining stems may reach 12 feet, decked out in broadly oval, 7-inch-long, glossy dark green leaves. With a bit of frost, leaves and stems may be nipped, but plants will recover when weather warms. In late summer, stems are adorned with flattish clusters of white buds that look like tiny paper lanterns; these open into striking, three-lobed red flowers with prominent stamens.

Restrained and mannerly, bleeding heart glorybower is a good candidate for decorating a trellis or post. It also grows well in large containers—useful when you want a portable screen, and convenient if you need to move the plant to shelter in winter.

CLYTOSTOMA callistegioides
VIOLET TRUMPET VINE
🌿 EVERGREEN 🍂 ZONES 9, 12–28

Clytostoma callistegioides

Pergolas and arbors find a near-perfect adornment in this rampant yet graceful vine. Just guide its stems up and over; their streamers of young growth will spill down from the arbor's edges to sway in the breeze. Wavy-margined, 3-inch leaves make a dense foliage cover on a vine that can reach 30 feet. Starting in mid- to late spring, trumpet-shaped violet, lavender, or pale purple flowers to 3 inches long and wide appear in small clusters; the peak show lasts about a month, with more modest displays continuing into fall. This vine climbs by tendrils (which appear on its leaves, not its stems); a wire support gives them a good purchase. Grown on a large, largely wire trellis, it makes a solid, almost hedgelike wall.

DISTICTIS
🌿 EVERGREEN 🍂 ZONES VARY BY SPECIES

Distictis buccinatoria

Many of the most spectacular (and most useful) subtropical vines have trumpet-shaped blossoms and are commonly called "trumpet vines." The three showoffs described here all radiate vigor and vitality, flaunting their conspicuous blooms on vines 20 to 30 feet long. Each leaf has two opposite oval leaflets and a central tendril that does the climbing.

Blood-red trumpet vine, *D. buccinatoria*, grows in Zones 8, 9, 14–28, where it produces numerous bursts of bloom throughout the growing season. Its 4-inch-long, yellow-throated trumpets open red orange, then age to rosy red. More restrained in growth is vanilla trumpet vine, *D. laxiflora*, suited to Zones 16, 22–27. It's named for the scent of its 3½-inch trumpets, which open violet, then age through lavender to white; flowers appear during the warmer months (March through October in the

Clematis, large-flowered hybrids
'Will Goodwin' and 'Ernest Markham'

CLIMBERS THAT TOLERATE SOME SHADE

Actinidia
Akebia quinata
Ampelopsis brevipedunculata
Aristolochia macrophylla
Beaumontia grandiflora
Bignonia capreolata
Clematis
Clerodendrum thomsoniae
Clytostoma callistegioides
Distictis
× *Fatshedera lizei*
Gelsemium sempervirens
Hardenbergia
Hibbertia scandens
Jasminum
Lapageria rosea
Lonicera
Macfadyena unguis-cati
Mandevilla
Pandorea
Passiflora
Podranea ricasoliana
Rosa (some)
Solanum jasminoides
Stephanotis floribunda
Trachelospermum jasminoides
Wisteria

mildest areas). Royal trumpet vine, *D.* 'Rivers' (sometimes sold as *D. riversii),* is a hybrid of the previous two species; like vanilla trumpet vine, it succeeds in Zones 16, 22–27. In vigor and foliage, it matches the *D. buccinatoria* parent, but its purple trumpets with orange throat markings are larger overall (to 5 inches).

Arbors display these vines nicely. On large trellises (preferably with wire for tendrils to wrap around), they'll form solid walls of leaves and flowers. They also make a handsome frosting for the top of a fence or wall if given narrow, horizontal trelliswork to climb along.

× Fatshedera lizei

× FATSHEDERA lizei

🌿 Evergreen 🌿 Zones 4–10, 12–31, warmer parts of 32

This unusual plant looks like the product of a science experiment with ivy—and that's what it is! The cross of vining English ivy *(Hedera helix)* with shrubby Japanese aralia *(Fatsia japonica)* produced an offspring just about midway between the parents—somewhat ivylike, somewhat vining, with thick but lax stems bearing 6- to 8-inch, glossy leaves with three to five pointed lobes. Unlike ivy, the plant does not extend indefinitely, nor does it attach itself to surfaces; stems branch little unless you pinch tips or cut them back. With a height or spread of about 10 feet, it makes a striking living sculpture on a wall or trellis; remember, though, that you'll need to tie it into place.

GELSEMIUM sempervirens
CAROLINA JESSAMINE
🌿 Evergreen 🌿 Zones 8–24, 26–33

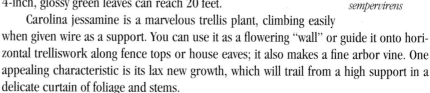

Any plant that flowers in winter is worth a second look, and this vine is handsome enough to hold its own in any season. Depending on winter cold, small clusters of flowers cover the foliage in midwinter to early spring—bright yellow, 1½-inch funnels that throw in a fine fragrance as a bonus. If you prefer blossoms with a fluffier look, choose the double-flowered variety 'Pride of Augusta' (sometimes sold as 'Plena'). Twining stems clothed in oval, 1- to 4-inch, glossy green leaves can reach 20 feet.

Gelsemium sempervirens

Carolina jessamine is a marvelous trellis plant, climbing easily when given wire as a support. You can use it as a flowering "wall" or guide it onto horizontal trelliswork along fence tops or house eaves; it also makes a fine arbor vine. One appealing characteristic is its lax new growth, which will trail from a high support in a delicate curtain of foliage and stems.

Note: All parts of Carolina jessamine are toxic if ingested.

Hardenbergia comptoniana

HARDENBERGIA
🌿 Evergreen 🌿 Zones vary by species

Their growth is distinctly more restrained—but in other respects, these purple-flowered evergreen vines might pass for wisteria. They even bloom in wisteria season, producing narrow, drooping clusters of sweet pea–like blossoms in late winter or early spring. The more cold-tolerant species is *H. violacea,* adapted to Zones 8–24; it's a dense twiner to about 10 feet, outfitted in 4-inch, lance-shaped leaves. The flowers may be violet, lilac, pink, or white; named varieties include pink-blossomed 'Rosea' and the somewhat larger-growing 'Happy Wanderer', with pinkish purple flowers. Lilac vine, *H. comptoniana*, grows in Zones 15–24; it's similar in size and habit to *H. violacea*, but has three-leafleted leaves that give it a finer-textured look. Despite the common name, its blooms are not lilac, but a vivid blue violet.

Their modest size and appealing blossoms suit these two vines to posts, trellises, and small arbors (or just part of a larger one). You can also train them on horizontal trellises, where they'll form a colorful ruffle along the top of a wall or fence.

HIBBERTIA scandens
GUINEA GOLD VINE
🌿 EVERGREEN ✿ ZONES 16, 17, 21–24

Within its preferred mild-winter regions, this vine's modest size, good-looking foliage, and long-lasting bloom put it into any "top five vines" list. Twining reddish brown stems extend to about 10 feet, adorned with glossy, oval leaves to 4 inches long. Sparkling against this polished background are lemon yellow, 3-inch flowers like single roses; bloom starts in midspring and peaks in summer, then continues (though less lavishly) into fall.

Let Guinea gold vine dress up a pillar, trellis, or small arbor. In the warmer parts of its range, it appreciates a bit of light afternoon shade; keep it away from south- or west-facing walls, where reflected heat is most intense.

Hibbertia scandens

HUMULUS lupulus
COMMON HOP
🌿 DECIDUOUS ✿ ZONES 11–24, 28–45

Grow your own beer! Well, grow the plant that provides the beer *flavoring*. For centuries, hops have been cultivated for their conelike flower heads, an essential ingredient in the brewing industry. In the home garden, common hop is an uncommonly attractive vine. Easy to grow and and easy to maintain, it has twining stems that grow rapidly from perennial roots to a height of 15 to 25 feet; hand-size, typically three-lobed leaves overlap like shingles as the plant gains height. Leaves of the basic species are a refreshing bright green, but the more ornamental 'Aureus' has foliage of a striking golden chartreuse. Bloom time comes in late summer. The true flowers are tiny, but they're enclosed in conspicuous clusters of bracts that resemble tiny, soft, pale green pine cones. When frosty weather arrives, leaves and stems are killed to the ground.

For an easy climb, give this vine wire (or even string) on which to twine. Try it on a wall trellis or a pillar; or train it up a freestanding trellis for a living green (or gold) wall. Before new stems start to grow in spring, remove the previous year's dead stems from the support.

Pillars make first-rate supports
for thriving *Humulus lupulus* 'Aureus'.

Humulus lupulus 'Aureus'

ABOVE: Sweet pea
RIGHT: Black-eyed Susan vine

ANNUAL VINES

The annual vines profiled here are long-time favorites of country and cottage gardens, cherished for their abundant color and ease of growth. Culture is simplicity itself: all you do is plant the seeds in a sunny spot, set up a support for climbing, and provide routine garden care. When bloom tapers off, strip the plants from their supports and wait for the next seed-planting time.

Most of these plants are twiners that do best with wirework trellises; larger growers (such as cup-and-saucer vine and morning glory) are suitable for covering smaller arbors. Nasturtiums and sweet peas flower during cool weather and are stopped by heat. The remaining choices described here reach their peak in summer; in colder-winter regions, some of them (as noted) should be started indoors, so they'll be ready for outdoor planting as soon as frost danger is past.

BLACK-EYED SUSAN VINE *(Thunbergia alata)*. Widely flaring, inch-wide trumpets of vivid orange with black throats adorn a 10-foot vine decked out in triangular leaves. Seed companies sometimes offer yellow- or white-flowered varieties; for solid orange blossoms, look for orange clock vine *(T. gregorii)*. Start seeds indoors in cold-winter regions. Plants are perennial in Zones 23–27.

CUP-AND-SAUCER VINE *(Cobaea scandens)*. The petals are united in a 2-inch, chalice-shaped "cup" mounted on a circle of green sepals—the "saucer." In the usual form, cups open green and progress to purple, but 'Alba' has white cups. The vigorous vine climbs by leaf tendrils to 25 feet, clinging not only to string and wire but even to rough surfaces. It's a better bet where the growing season is long and warm. In cool-summer regions, bloom won't begin until late summer—and where the growing season is short, even plants started indoors may not reach flowering size before frost. In all but the mildest zones, start seeds indoors. Plants are perennial in Zones 24–27.

Cup-and-saucer vine

GOURDS. Though gourd vines produce showy yellow flowers resembling those of squash, the hard-shelled, decorative fruits are the real draw: round, bottle shaped, crooknecked, curved, or coiled, in a range of sizes and surface markings. The vines have sandpapery stems and leaves (again, like those of squash) and reach a vigorous

Gourds

10 to 15 feet. Several different types are widely sold. *Cucurbita pepo ovifera* bears small fruits in a variety of shapes. *Lagenaria siceraria* has white flowers that develop into fruits of various shapes to 3 feet long; *Luffa aegyptica* produces cylindrical fruits with a fibrous interior that can be dried and used as a bath sponge. Start seeds indoors in all but mild-winter regions.

Morning glory Early Call

MORNING GLORY *(Ipomoea)*. Two annual species offer the familiar funnel-shaped flowers and heart-shaped leaves on vigorous vines to about 15 feet. *I. tricolor* 'Heavenly Blue' is the long-time favorite, with 4- to 5-inch blossoms of the traditional sky blue. Also available are white-flowered varieties and mixed-color strains including pink, crimson, purple, and lavender. *I. nil* includes the large-flowered Imperial Japanese morning glories (with blossoms to 6 inches across) as well as red 'Scarlett O'Hara', pinkish brown 'Chocolate', and the mixed-color Early Call strain. In cold-winter regions, start seeds indoors.

Morning glory
'Heavenly Blue'

NASTURTIUM *(Tropaeolum majus)*. Its large seeds, fast growth, and bright flowers make this one a favorite with children. Leaves and flowers are edible, adding a tangy accent to salads. The thick-stemmed vines climb by coiling leafstalks to about 6 feet high, providing a dense cover of long-stalked, nearly circular leaves. The 3-inch, five-lobed flowers are shallowly cup shaped, with a spur in back; the prevailing colors are yellow and orange, but you'll also find strains with blossoms in red, maroon, and creamy white. In the mildest-winter zones, plant seeds in fall for bloom in winter and spring (and into summer, if weather stays cool enough); elsewhere, plant in late winter or early spring.

Nasturtium

SWEET PEA *(Lathyrus odoratus)*. The plant itself has no special beauty—it's just a typical pea plant—but the masses of ruffled, silky-petaled, gloriously fragrant flowers are breathtaking. Colors include pastels (white, cream, lavender, pink) and deeper hues of violet and red; some varieties even have bicolored or multicolored blossoms. All sweet peas need good soil. The standard sorts also need cool temperatures during the flowering period, so time your plantings to take advantage of the longest possible stretch of cool weather. Where winters are mild and summers hot, the best tactic is to plant in fall for winter and spring bloom. In areas with cool winters and warm to hot summers, spring-flowering strains are successful. Where winters are long and cold and summers warm but not hot, look for summer-flowering strains.

Sweet pea

Sweet pea

Jasminum polyanthum

JASMINUM

JASMINE

🌿 EVERGREEN, SEMIEVERGREEN, AND DECIDUOUS ✦ ZONES VARY BY SPECIES

So closely connected are jasmines and fragrance that a number of unrelated but highly perfumed plants include the word "jasmine" in their common name; *Mandevilla laxa* (page 46), *Stephanotis floribunda* (page 51), and *Trachelospermum jasminoides* (page 51) are just three examples. Among the true jasmines, you'll find a number of twining vines that offer clusters of pinwheel-shaped, 1-inch white flowers with the legendary scent. Here are five of the most popular.

Spanish jasmine, *J. grandiflorum,* and common white jasmine, *J. officinale,* are generally similar but for their size: the former reaches about 15 feet, while the latter can grow twice as large. Both are summer bloomers suited to Zones 5–9, 12–24, 28, 29, and 31. Rich green leaves are composed of narrow leaflets that make a fine-textured foliage mass; the vines are semievergreen in their warmer zones, deciduous in the colder ones. Angelwing jasmine, *J. nitidum,* grows only in Zones 12, 13, 16, 19–21, and 26. It's a 10- to 20-foot vine with 3-inch, glossy leaves; foliage is evergreen or semievergreen, depending on winter cold. Strongly fragrant flowers come in late spring and summer, opening from purple buds.

Two evergreen jasmines give you flowers from late winter into spring. The hardier of the two, *J. polyanthum,* grows in Zones 5–9, 12–24, 28, and 31. An exuberant 20-footer, it's covered in almost fernlike foliage; the rose-backed blossoms give plants in full bloom an overall pinkish tinge. Downy jasmine, *J. multiflorum,* is a 15-foot vine suited to Zones 21–24, 26, and 28. Its blossoms are just lightly perfumed; a downy coating on the 2-inch leaves gives the foliage a soft gray-green cast.

These easy-to-grow jasmines climb best if given some sort of wire trelliswork, on which their stems can quickly twine upward. Guided up and over arbors and pergolas, they'll produce a light-textured froth of foliage and flowers; on a trellis, they'll form a solid cover.

Lapageria rosea

LAPAGERIA rosea

CHILEAN BELLFLOWER

🌿 EVERGREEN
✦ ZONES 5, 6, 15–17, 23, 24

This elegant vine needs a bit of extra care, but your efforts will be well rewarded: small clusters of pendent, 3-inch bells appear over a long spring-to-fall bloom period, their petals so thick and waxy they look almost like the products of a sculptor's workshop. The usual color is dark rosy red (often spotted with white), but pink and pure white variants sometimes are sold. Stems twine to 20 feet at most, outfitted (but not covered) in glossy, thick-textured, oval leaves to 4 inches long.

Success with Chilean bellflower depends on good, well-drained soil amended with plenty of organic matter; vines also need a lightly shaded location protected from wind. In a sheltered patio or outdoor-living area, Chilean bellflower makes a lovely display on a trellis or post. Or use it to decorate one corner of an arbor or pergola.

Lonicera × brownii

LONICERA
HONEYSUCKLE

Evergreen, semievergreen, and deciduous
Zones vary by species

With one conspicuous exception, the honeysuckles project a country charm: they're pretty but not elegant or flamboyant, eager to grow but a bit disheveled at times, and often endowed with a scent that recalls cottage gardens and pastoral walks. All bear modest clusters of flowers on twining stems clothed with oval leaves in opposing pairs. The basic flower form is a slender tube, but in many of the most familiar honeysuckles, the tube flares into two unequal pairs of lobes.

As five of the six species described below attest, most honeysuckles adapt to a wide range of climates; most thrive in a broad range of soil types, too. Given their vigor and tendency to tangle, they're best suited to larger arbors and pergolas; for trellis or pillar training, choose *L. × brownii*, *L. × heckrottii*, or *L. japonica* 'Aureoreticulata'.

Deciduous *L. × brownii* is the most cold-tolerant species, growing in Zones 1–7, 31–45. Its variety 'Dropmore Scarlet' bears tubular orange-red (but unscented) flowers from late spring into fall, on vines to about 10 feet. Nearly as hardy is Japanese honeysuckle, *L. japonica*, suited to Zones 2–41. It is evergreen in warmer zones, semievergreen to fully deciduous in colder-winter areas. The rampant vines easily reach 30 feet, producing white, strongly fragrant blooms of flaring-tubular form from late spring into fall. The variety 'Halliana' (Hall's honeysuckle) is widely grown; its flowers open white and age to tawny yellow. 'Purpurea' has purple leaf undersides and purple-backed petals. 'Aureoreticulata', goldnet honeysuckle, is a considerably smaller vine with green leaves completely netted in yellow veining.

Another species hardy in Zones 2–41 is trumpet honeysuckle, *L. sempervirens*. It's deciduous in all but the mildest-winter regions, where some foliage remains year-round. From midspring into summer, the 20-foot vine bears orange-red, unscented, flaring tubes; named selections include yellow-flowered 'Sulphurea' ('Flava') and several varieties with red blossoms.

TOP: *Lonicera japonica* 'Aureoreticulata'
BOTTOM: *Lonicera periclymenum*

Woodbine, *L. periclymenum*, grows in Zones 2–24, 30–41. It resembles a smaller (to 20-foot) version of Japanese honeysuckle, with the added attraction of berrylike red fruits in fall. A number of named varieties are sold. 'Serotina' and 'Belgica' have flowers that are purple outside, yellow inside; blooms of 'Serotina Florida' are red outside, cream within. Yellow flowers of 'Berries Jubilee' are followed by a heavy crop of red fruits. Vigorous 'Graham Thomas' grows to 30 feet, producing pale cream flowers that age to tawny yellow.

Lonicera sempervirens

Gold flame honeysuckle, *L. × heckrottii*, grows in Zones 3–24, 30–45. Its moderately fragrant flowers of flaring-tube form are rose pink on the outside, yellow inside; they bloom from spring into fall on a semievergreen to deciduous plant that reaches only about 15 feet.

Giant Burmese honeysuckle, *L. hildebrandiana*, is a striking departure from the preceding five species. Its flowers are like those of Japanese honeysuckle in shape, color, and scent, but can reach 7 inches in length; the thick, ropelike stems, clothed in 6-inch evergreen leaves, twine to 30 feet. This is the least cold-tolerant species, growing only in Zones 9, 14–17, 19–28.

Lonicera × heckrottii

MACFADYENA unguis-cati
CAT'S CLAW, YELLOW TRUMPET VINE
EVERGREEN TO DECIDUOUS ✿ ZONES 8–29, 31

If you need a shaded patio in a hurry, build an overhead and plant a cat's claw vine. Its forked tendrils will climb anything but smooth surfaces, and its stems quickly grow to 40 feet or more. It's pretty, too: glossy light green, 2-inch, oval leaflets form a dense background for a springtime show of 4-inch-wide, trumpetlike blossoms in bright lemon yellow. Plants are evergreen in the warmest zones, almost entirely deciduous as you move into colder territory.

VINES WITH MODERATE WATER NEEDS

Ampelopsis brevipedunculata
Clytostoma callistegioides
Lonicera
Macfadyena unguis-cati
Pandorea
Passiflora
Podranea ricasoliana
Polygonum
Pyrostegia venusta
Solanum jasminoides
Tecomaria capensis
Vitis
Wisteria

MANDEVILLA
EVERGREEN, SEMIEVERGREEN, AND DECIDUOUS
✿ ZONES VARY BY SPECIES

Mandevilla splendens

Given their preferred good, well-drained, organically enriched soil, these twining vines radiate robust health. All have showy trumpet-shaped flowers and abundant glossy foliage.

Chilean jasmine, *M. laxa,* is a summer bloomer that grows in Zones 4–9, 14–21, 28, 29, and 31; it's evergreen, semievergreen, or deciduous, depending on the depth of winter cold. The common name alludes to the fragrance of the 2-inch, trumpet-shaped white blossoms, though the perfume is in fact closer to gardenia than jasmine. The vine twines to 15 feet or more, providing a dense cover of narrowly heart-shaped, 6-inch leaves. New growth is red purple; leaves may turn bronzy red in fall.

The other mandevillas are evergreen and strictly for warm-winter territory. Pink allamanda, *M. splendens,* and its hybrid offspring *M.* 'Alice du Pont' grow in Zones 21–25. These two are so similar as to be interchangeable: both have glossy, oval leaves to 8 inches long and red-throated hot pink flowers to 4 inches across. Named selections of *M. splendens* include 'My Fair Lady' (pink-blushed white), 'Red Riding Hood' (dark reddish pink), and 'Scarlet Pimpernel' (yellow-throated dark red). The flowers bloom from spring into fall, carried on vines that reach 20 feet or more in favored locations.

Tenderest of all the mandevillas is *M. boliviensis,* which grows only in Zones 24 and 25. It reaches 12 to 20 feet, its stems clothed in pointed, 4-inch leaves. Yellow-throated white trumpets to 3 inches across bloom throughout the year; 'Summer Snow' has pink-tinged white flowers.

Chilean jasmine is beautiful on arbors, pergolas, and large, stout trellises. The other mandevillas described above are particularly fine trained to trellises or pillars; they also grow well in containers (though they'll be smaller than in-ground vines).

PANDOREA
EVERGREEN; ✿ ZONES 16–27

Some plants are best kept out of sight after flowering—but these two twining vines have such attractive foliage it would hardly matter if they never bloomed. Fortunately, though, they offer you the complete package. Bower vine, *P. jasminoides,* is the smaller

Pandorea jasminoides 'Rosea'

of the two (to about 20 feet), but it bears larger flowers. Foliage is a rich glossy green, with each leaf consisting of up to nine pointed-oval leaflets to 2 inches long. Clusters of trumpet-shaped, 2-inch-wide flowers appear from late spring into early fall. The typical flower is white with a pink throat, but 'Alba' and 'Lady D' bear pure white blossoms, while 'Rosea' offers soft pink flowers with a red throat. Wonga-wonga vine, *P. pandorana*, is about twice the size of bower vine, but the 1 to 3-inch-long leaflets are narrower. Trumpetlike flowers just under an inch across come in pinkish to creamy white.

Each vine's size dictates its best uses. Bower vine is excellent on posts and trellises; locate it where it will be protected from strong wind. Wonga-wonga vine is a fine adornment for an arbor where you want a full, leafy cover.

PASSIFLORA
PASSION FLOWER
🌿 Evergreen, semievergreen, and deciduous 🔆 Zones vary by species

Pandorea pandorana

Spanish missionaries of several hundred years ago found religious imagery in these intricately fashioned flowers, hence the common name. Today, though, the blossoms are more likely to elicit reactions along the lines "oh, my" and "how beautiful!" The petals and sepals are virtually identical in appearance, spread out starlike in a flat plane; a corona of wavy, threadlike filaments lies atop them, and rising from the blossom center is a pedestal-like structure containing the reproductive parts. (To the missionaries, the lacy corona represented the crown of thorns; the five stamens, the five wounds; and the 10 petals and sepals, the 10 faithful apostles.) Many species bear egg-shaped edible fruits. The plentiful foliage is medium to coarse in texture; leaves are often lobed.

Climbing by tendrils, these vines are vigorous: most charge ahead rampantly to 30 feet or so. They are ideal on pergolas and large arbors, where they can spread with abandon. You can also display them on large trellises against walls or fences, but their dense and tangling growth will require periodic attention if it is to remain neat.

Many of the passion flowers come from tropical and near-tropical climates and will grow only in completely frost-free regions. The following widely available sorts, however, are fairly cold tolerant. All but *P. × alatocaerulea* bear edible fruits; all bloom in summer unless otherwise noted.

Passiflora caerulea

Passiflora incarnata

Maypop or wild passion vine, *P. incarnata*, is a Southeastern native suited to Zones 4–10, 12–33; it is deciduous in warmer zones but dies to the ground in colder areas. The 3-inch flowers are white to pale lilac, with a pink-and-purple corona. This species' hybrid *P.* 'Incense' grows in Zones 5–31; like its parent, it is a deciduous vine that dies back in the coldest regions. Flowers are violet with a paler corona; they reach 5 inches across and have a perfume like that of sweet peas.

Another species and its hybrid grow in Zones 5–9, 12–29. Both retain all or most leaves in warmer zones, die to the ground in colder regions. Blue crown passion flower, *P. caerulea*, blooms from summer to fall, bearing 2- to 4-inch, greenish white flowers with purple coronas. Its hybrid *P. × alatocaerulea* has 4-inch, white-and-purple blossoms with a striking deep purple corona.

PODRANEA ricasoliana
PINK TRUMPET VINE
🌿 EVERGREEN TO DECIDUOUS 🍂 ZONES 9, 12, 13, 19–27

Though by no means lacking in vigor, this vine won't assault an arbor with jungle-generating exuberance. Its twining stems grow at a moderate rate to about 20 feet, carrying glossy leaves composed of oval, 2-inch leaflets. The floral display comes in summer, when the stems are decorated with elongated clusters of blossoms like asymmetrical trumpets to 2 inches across; the color is a warm pink, with red lines extending into a yellow throat. In frost-free regions, foliage is attractive all year. Light frosts can cause leaves to drop; heavier frosts may kill stems to the ground, but regrowth should occur in spring.

Pink trumpet vine provides a refined accent on pillars and smaller arbors. Try it on a trellis against a sunny wall, where it will revel in the warmth it prefers.

*Podranea
ricasoliana*

POLYGONUM
🌿 EVERGREEN TO DECIDUOUS 🍂 ZONES VARY BY SPECIES

Two nearly identical vines combine the toughness of steel wool and the delicacy of cotton candy. In their central Asian homeland, they thrive in heat, cold, and indifferent soil, and their tolerance for such less-than-ideal conditions recommends them for problem areas where fussier vines might fail. They're popular in seaside and arid regions, and ideal for smothering blots on the landscape—derelict sheds, ugly fences, abandoned cars. But they're far too attractive to be relegated to just these uses. Common to both species are thin, wiry, twining stems with wavy-edged, 2½-inch, heart-shaped leaves. Tiny, fragrant flowers are carried in large, dense, elongated clusters; from late spring into fall, they cover the vines in a floral froth. Even in cold-winter areas, plants can reach 20 feet in a single growing season, and in warmer zones they may attain twice that size.

Silver lace vine, *P. aubertii,* grows in Zones 2–24, 28–41; foliage ranges from evergreen in the warmest areas to deciduous in the coldest spots. Flowers are pure white. Bokhara fleece flower, *P. baldschuanicum,* grows in Zones 2–24, 31–41. Also called mile-a-minute vine, it differs from silver lace vine only in slightly larger flowers that turn pinkish with age.

Given their ultimate size and unstoppable vigor, these vines are not for trellises—unless you have a huge one that covers a two-story wall! Pergolas and large arbors provide the perfect setting, letting the vines grow and billow at will as they provide shade and bloom.

Polygonum aubertii

Pyrostegia venusta

PYROSTEGIA venusta
FLAME VINE
🌿 EVERGREEN 🍂 ZONES 13, 16, 21–27

This robust climber seems to set the garden afire in winter, when color is at especially welcome. Large, drooping clusters of 3-inch, orange, honeysucklelike blossoms are carried aloft on a rampant vine to 20 feet or more; flowering may start in fall (in the warmest areas) and continue into spring. Stems climb by twining and by leaf tendrils.

In keeping with the "flame" of the common name, this plant does best in warmer areas and languishes in coolness and shade. It is a perfect candidate for a large trellis against a warm wall or fence. It also makes a striking statement on an arbor, from which the orange blossoms can spill like a flow of molten lava.

ROSA
ROSE

🌿 Evergreen and deciduous ⚘ Zones vary by species

Rosa 'Wind Chimes'

Climbing roses are the most widely planted of all flowering vines, and it's easy to see why: not only are they beautiful, they're inescapable! With every year, retail nurseries and specialty mail-order firms include more climbers among their countless rose offerings, a surge due both to the efforts of current rose breeders and to the increased availability of climbing heritage and species roses.

Climbing roses are a varied lot, ranging from modest plants to decorate a pillar or trellis to rampant behemoths that can smother a pergola or cover a two-story wall. Species roses and some heritage types mount just one lavish spring display per year, but the majority of modern climbers flower repeatedly from spring into fall. All climbing roses must be tied to their supports; their thorns help them climb by hooking into other growth but offer no secure attachment.

These roses vary in cold tolerance. Climbing Noisettes, teas, and the evergreen species *R. banksiae* and *R. laevigata* (see below) are the most cold sensitive, performing best in Zones 4–9, 12–31. At the other end of the scale are certain modern climbers such as the Canadian Explorer roses, which were developed expressly to withstand northern winters with a minimum of damage to exposed canes. The majority of climbing roses, however, will go undamaged through winter in Zones 4–32; in colder regions, some protection is usually needed to prevent damage or death from freezes.

The next four paragraphs offer a brief sketch of the various types of climbing roses. For fuller descriptions of these classes (and of superior varieties in each), and for pruning guidelines, consult *Sunset's Roses* (1998).

Rosa 'America'

SPECIES. A number of rose species are large plants with arching canes that can be left to sprawl as shrubs or tied to a trellis and grown as climbers. In addition to these, you'll find various truly climbing kinds with very long, flexible canes. Two such species are *R. banksiae* (banksia rose) and *R. laevigata* (Cherokee rose); both are big, virtually evergreen climbers for mild-winter regions.

HERITAGE ROSES. Among the spring-blooming old European classes, the alba, centifolia, and moss roses include varieties rangy and supple enough to be trained as restrained climbers. The China, Bourbon, Noisette, tea, and hybrid perpetual classes include repeat-flowering, truly climbing roses.

RAMBLERS. The roses known as ramblers produce long, slender, flexible canes that are easily trained to trellises and arbors. They flower mainly in spring, then typically produce much new growth that must be tied into place or thinned out.

MODERN ROSES. Almost without exception, these roses flower repeatedly throughout the growing season. The best-known modern class is the hybrid tea; the many climbers in this group include natural climbers (some of which are classified as LCL—large-flowered climber) as well as climbing sports of popular bush varieties. Other modern groups such as grandiflora and floribunda also feature climbing sports of bush varieties. Even among modern shrub roses (particularly the hybrid musks and the group marketed as English roses), you'll find individuals that produce essentially climbing canes in the milder-winter regions of the West, South, and Southeast.

Solandra maxima 'Variegata'

SOLANDRA maxima
CUP-OF-GOLD VINE
Evergreen ✿ Zones 17, 21–25, 26 (southern part), 27

This striking vine combines tropical luxuriance with an almost alien beauty. A single plant can reach 40 feet if not cut back by frost or pruning shears. Vines are thick stemmed, with a moderately dense foliage cover of highly polished, broadly oval leaves to 6 inches long. Long, puffy buds open to enormous blossoms—great leathery-textured, five-lobed chalices of banana yellow aging to chamois, with a red-brown stripe running down each lobe to the flower center. Bloom is most profuse from winter into early spring, but blossoms can appear in lesser quantity throughout the rest of the year. Rare selection 'Variegata' has leaves edged in creamy white.

Grow cup-of-gold vine where it will be sheltered from frost and wind. A sizable arbor or pergola displays it to advantage; a large trellis on a warm wall provides a spectacular showcase. You also can train the vine on narrow, horizontal trelliswork along wall tops and house eaves. Training is needed in any situation, since the stems are not self-attaching and must be tied into place.

SOLANUM
Evergreen to deciduous ✿ Zones vary by species

Solanum jasminoides

The vining *Solanum* species are for milder-winter areas only. Within these limits, they can be divided into those that tolerate some frost and those that won't take even the lightest touch. All have clusters of yellow-centered, starlike, typically inch-wide blossoms that proclaim the vines' kinship to potatoes and tomatoes.

Two frost-tolerant species grow in Zones 8, 9, 12–27. Evergreen to semievergreen potato vine, *S. jasminoides,* twines as far as 30 feet, forming a tangle of slender stems, arrowhead-shaped leaves, and clustered white blossoms. The vine is covered in a froth of bloom in spring, and flowering continues (though less profusely) into the summer months. Evergreen *S. crispum,* too, has slender stems—but they don't twine and reach only about 12 feet. The fragrant, lavender-blue summer flowers are followed by pealike yellow fruits. For darker flowers in larger clusters, look for 'Glasnevin'.

Gardeners in Zones 16, 21–25 can grow two tropical species. Evergreen to semievergreen Brazilian nightshade, *S. seaforthianum,* is a 15-footer with slender, nontwining stems and oval to lobed leaves; summer flowers of vivid violet blue are followed by small red fruits that attract birds. Deciduous Costa Rican nightshade, *S. wendlandii,* reaches 15 to 20 feet, climbing by twining and by hooked spines. Rounded clusters of 2½-inch, lavender-blue blossoms put on a striking summer show.

Where adapted, these vines are easy to grow and offer plenty of fresh-looking color; those with blue blooms are particularly effective in the summer landscape. All are fine plants for trellis and pillar training, and potato vine and Costa Rican nightshade are large enough for arbors as well. Remember that both *S. crispum* and Brazilian nightshade will require tying to any support. Give potato vine and *S. crispum* a bit of afternoon shade in hot-summer regions.

Solanum crispum

STEPHANOTIS floribunda
MADAGASCAR JASMINE

EVERGREEN / ZONES 23–25

Only frost sensitivity limits the popularity of this elegant and restrained vine. Lucky gardeners in the warmest zones can revel in its intoxicatingly fragrant blossoms (a staple in bridal bouquets), borne on a vine that twines to 15 to 25 feet. Carried in clusters of up to nine, the waxy white, tubular flowers open into 1½-inch stars; the leaves are leathery, 2- to 4-inch ovals. The peak flowering period comes in summer, with scattered bloom in other months.

In its favored frost-free zones, use Madagascar jasmine to decorate an obelisk, small arbor, or trellis, preferably in an outdoor-living area where you can savor the heady perfume. In slightly colder zones where light frost is an occasional hazard, try growing the vine on a trellis in a large container which can be moved to shelter when freezes threaten.

Stephanotis floribunda

TECOMARIA capensis
CAPE HONEYSUCKLE

EVERGREEN / ZONES 12, 13, 16, 18–28

Hot-summer gardeners, check out this vine! It actually prefers high temperatures, and it looks fresh and healthy even when less heat-tolerant plants are visibly pining for cooler weather. It has no means of attachment, but it's tractable: you can tie the stems into place to suit yourself. The vine can reach 15 to 25 feet. Leaves of a rich, glossy green are composed of up to nine broadly oval leaflets; clusters of 2-inch, honeysuckle-type blossoms can appear from late summer into winter. Vibrant red orange is the standard flower color, but a clear yellow variety, 'Aurea', also is available.

Cape honeysuckle presents no cultural challenges, and once established, it can get by with considerably less than regular watering. Use it on trellises (especially against warm walls), arbors, pergolas—anywhere its vivid blossoms can be shown off to advantage.

Tecomaria capensis

TRACHELOSPERMUM jasminoides
STAR JASMINE, CONFEDERATE JASMINE

EVERGREEN / ZONES 8–31, WARMEST PARTS OF 32

Even some jasmines might envy this vine's perfume—and it offers much more than an intoxicating scent. Foliage is good looking, too: a dense cloak of oval, leathery, 3-inch leaves that unfurl a glossy pale green, then mature to a much darker shade. Happy in sun or shade, the vine ascends by twining stems to 20 feet if given suitable support. Clusters of white, inch-wide, pinwheel-shaped blossoms appear in summer in cooler zones, in mid- to late spring where winters are mild. For variety in foliage, look for 'Variegatum', with leaves bordered and blotched in white.

Given good soil and regular watering, star jasmine grows vigorously. It's an excellent trellis candidate for a prominent garden spot where you need a year-round neat appearance. It also makes a nice display on pillars (given some attachment for twining) and small arbors.

Trachelospermum jasminoides

Vitis

CLIMBERS WITH DECORATIVE FRUIT

Actinidia deliciosa

Akebia quinata

Ampelopsis brevipedunculata

Passiflora

Rosa

Pyrostegia venusta

Rosa

Solanum crispum

Solanum seaforthianum

Vitis

No support is too large or too massive for big, vigorous wisteria vines.

VITIS
GRAPE

🌿 DECIDUOUS ✀ ZONES VARY BY SPECIES

Like kiwi (*Actinidia deliciosa,* page 34), grapes can be used strictly ornamentally or planted for fruit. Either way, you get vigorous vines that can cover considerable territory, extending their reach by means of tightly coiling tendrils. The roughly circular, shallowly to deeply lobed leaves are large—often virtually hand size. Most offer fall color, turning to vivid yellow, orange, red, or maroon depending on the species and, to some extent, on the autumn weather.

Grapes fall into three broad categories: table grapes (used for eating fresh and for preserves), wine grapes, and purely ornamental grapes with good-looking foliage but fruit that isn't good enough for eating or winemaking. Any of these can be informally trained to cover a pergola or large arbor (these two are the best support structures for them). If you want a reliable fruit crop, though, you'll need to choose a variety adapted to your climate, then train and prune it according to specific guidelines. For pruning information and a description of grape varieties, consult *Sunset's National Garden Book.*

A particularly notable ornamental grape is *V. coignetiae,* sometimes called crimson glory vine in reference to its fall foliage (and leaves turn not only crimson, but orange and coppery as well). In Zones 3–10, 14–21, 28–41, the vine grows rampantly to 50 feet or more, outfitted in foot-long, lightly lobed leaves.

WISTERIA

🌿 DECIDUOUS ✀ ZONES VARY BY SPECIES

For elegance, grace, and sophistication, the wisterias are without peer. In early spring, the vines are covered in a fragrant veil of bloom: long, narrow, pendent clusters of sweet pea–like blossoms in violet, lavender, white, or pink. These are succeeded by languid, feathery leaves composed of paired, tapered leaflets that turn a pleasing yellow or gold in fall. In time, vines become quite picturesque—the main trunks and limbs attain an arm-thick girth and a covering of almost muscular-looking grayish tan bark.

Japanese and Chinese wisterias are the sorts most commonly sold, since they offer the most lavish floral displays. Japanese wisteria, *W. floribunda,* grows in Zones 2–24, 26, 28–41. Its stems twine clockwise. Leaves can reach 16 inches long (each containing up to 19 leaflets); blossom clusters are in the 1- to 1½-foot range. Fragrant flowers typically open first at the top of the cluster, then proceed downward toward its tip. The standard color is light to medium violet, but named varieties give you specific color choices. For double flowers in a mid-lavender shade, try 'Violacea Plena'; for extremely long blossom clusters (some recorded at over 3 feet in length), look for 'Macrobotrys' ('Longissima').

Chinese wisteria, *W. sinensis* (Zones 3–24, 26, 28–35, 37, and 39), has smaller blossom clusters than those of Japanese wisteria (to about 1 foot), and all the flowers open almost simultaneously. Leaves are smaller too (to about 1 foot long, each with up to 13 leaflets); stems twine counterclockwise. Seed-grown plants, often labeled simply "Chinese wisteria," may take years to come into bloom; for bloom at an earlier age and a guarantee of flower color and quality, named varieties are a better bet.

Wisteria vines are exuberant growers that become quite heavy as they mature—a point to remember in providing support. They're ideal showpieces for large overheads and pergolas. If you want to display them against a large wall, choose a husky trellis and anchor it firmly to the wall. Chinese wisteria will bloom in sun or partial shade. For Japanese wisteria, always choose a sunny spot; it won't produce flowers in shade.

Vines with Showy Flowers

Beautiful foliage is a fine adornment for a trellis or arbor, but flowers add an extra measure of enjoyment. Here are a number of garden favorites, listed according to their seasons of bloom.

Clytostoma callistegioides

SPRING

Akebia quinata
Beaumontia grandiflora
Bignonia capreolata
Bougainvillea
Clematis (some)
Clytostoma callistegioides
Distictis
Gelsemium sempervirens
Hardenbergia
Hibbertia scandens
Jasminum (some)
Lapageria rosea
Lonicera
Macfadyena unguis-cati
Mandevilla boliviensis
Mandevilla splendens
Pandorea
Passiflora (some)

Polygonum
Pyrostegia venusta
Rosa
Solandra maxima
Solanum jasminoides
Stephanotis floribunda
*Trachelospermum
    jasminoides*
Wisteria

SUMMER

Beaumontia grandiflora
Bougainvillea
Clematis (some)
*Clerodendrum
    thomsoniae*
Clytostoma callistegioides
Distictis
Hibbertia scandens
Jasminum (some)
Lapageria rosea
Lonicera
Mandevilla boliviensis
Mandevilla laxa
Mandevilla splendens
Pandorea
Passiflora (some)
Podranea
Polygonum
Rosa (some)
Solanum crispum
Solanum jasminoides
Solanum seaforthianum
Solanum wendlandii
Stephanotis floribunda
Tecomaria capensis
*Trachelospermum
    jasminoides*
Wisteria

AUTUMN

Bougainvillea
Clematis (some)
Distictis
Hibbertia scandens
Lapageria rosea
Lonicera
Mandevilla boliviensis
Mandevilla splendens
Pandorea
Passiflora (some)
Polygonum
Pyrostegia venusta
Rosa
Tecomaria capensis

WINTER

Gelsemium sempervirens
Hardenbergia
Jasminum (some)
Mandevilla boliviensis
Pyrostegia venusta
Solandra maxima
Tecomaria capensis
Wisteria

Bougainvillea

RIGHT: Established climbing rose functions as a trellis for purple-blossomed clematis hybrid.

You've discovered how vertical gardening can stretch your landscape skyward and frame or mask a view. Maybe you've found just the right vine for your backyard retreat. Now you

TRELLIS

PROJECTS

need the trellis. You could, of course, purchase a prefab trellis from a nursery or home supply center. But why not build your own? On the following pages, you'll encounter a broad palette of designs, from crisp, classic English grids through gnarled, rustic twig structures to vegetable cages and stylish movable screens. Some mount on a wall or fence; others are freestanding focal points.

Many of these trellises are quite simple to build, though a few are more complex. We begin with a look at basic components, then walk through the construction of a typical gridwork trellis. In many cases, the designs that follow are more suggestions than strict blueprints; they can be scaled up or down. The instructions assume you have some acquaintance with basic building techniques such as measuring, cutting, and fastening. If you need more help, turn to "Nuts and Bolts," beginning on page 95.

If you do decide to buy instead of build, first take a look at the shopping tips on pages 64–65.

A simple lath grid provides open, airy support for a clematis vine smothered in snowy white blooms.

TRELLIS-BUILDING BASICS

If you're thinking of making a trellis, especially one of your own design, it helps to bone up on a few basics. Though most trellis projects are easy, you'll still need the right combination of materials and techniques to ensure the best results. Of course, some trellis designs—notably contoured, sculptural shapes made from wrought iron or steel—may be better bought than bungled, unless you have metalworking skills. This caution is especially apt if your trellis will be part of a formal or artistic landscape. If you're inclined toward this sort of style, turn to pages 64–65 for shopping tips.

DESIGN OPTIONS

A trellis is essentially a two-dimensional frame for plants, made with verticals and horizontals that are fastened together. The traditional model is a rectangular wooden grid that gives plants a good foothold, allows air circulation, and holds itself together. But just about anything flat or round that stands up to the elements, supports the weight of mature plants, and can be nailed, screwed, or wired together can serve as a lightweight trellis, especially if it will be supported by a wall or fence.

With that said, remember that a trellis has more than a purely utilitarian role (after all, it's not always thickly covered with foliage and flowers). The design you choose should match the surroundings in style. Some trellises are elegantly symmetric; others are more rustic; some are unabashedly eclectic. Some designs advance, functioning as focal points, while others let plants steal the show. You'll find examples of all types on the following pages.

In many cases, you can convert a two-dimensional trellis to a three-dimensional arbor simply by building one or more additional frames that match the first, placing them parallel to each other, and bridging them with horizontal braces that create "walls" and a "roof." You'll see examples of this technique on pages 82–83.

The trellis's scale should suit its setting: a 2½-foot-high grid may overpower a small patio container, while even a 7-foot-tall tower can look small in the center of a large, open space. The landscape also determines how finished the trellis should look. A formal landscape may call for a trellis that's sanded, filled, rounded over, and painted to match the house trim; in more casual surroundings, a rough-redwood cage or a frame of lashed-together crooked branches may be right at home.

MATERIALS

Most trellises are made from milled wood: standard dimension lumber, lattice and lath, moldings, dowels, or tree stakes. The reasons? Wood is easy to work with; it's strong; plants seem to like it; and, if chosen and prepped properly, it should stand up to water, wind, and summer heat.

The most durable structures are made from naturally decay-resistant woods (such as redwood or cedar heartwoods) or from pressure-treated lumber. Most trellis pieces are light-weights—typically ½- by 1½-inch lath, 1 by 2s, 2 by 2s, and sometimes 2 by 4s. Occasionally, larger freestanding frames are held up with stout 4 by 4 posts or 6-inch-diameter poles. You can let redwood or cedar weather naturally, paint it, or seal it with an exterior finish (see page 106). Pressure-treated lumber can be hard to find in small sizes, and you'll probably want to paint it to conceal its typical greenish cast. For more on lumber and a definition of terms, see pages 96–97.

Most trellis joinery is simple. Butt joints are the norm; they are held together by nails, screws, or wire, and sometimes with waterproof glue as well. For a more formal look, some projects call for more intricate lap joints. You'll want rust-resistant, galvanized fasteners and hardware for these outdoor projects. For more on fasteners and joinery, see pages 98–99 and 103–104.

WHAT'S INVOLVED?

Building a basic wood trellis like the one shown on the facing page is pretty, well, basic—almost anyone can put one together in a day. The results needn't be perfect to be pleasing. You'll need some standard tools, such as a saw, measuring tape, and hammer and/or power drill with bits. Bigger structures take more time and more stamina, and you may need some extra hands to install them. For a closer look at trellis-making tools and techniques, see pages 100–105.

As is true for much carpentry, it's the frills and niceties that are most demanding. Lap joints and miter joints are more easily done with power tools. A router is handy for the rounded or chamfered edges that add a more finished look. Fortunately, the straightforward charm of most trellis designs means that they're easy to build, too.

BUILDING A BASIC TRELLIS

1   This traditional lath trellis is largely a matter of crisscrossing uprights and crosspieces. Lay the uprights on a flat surface, face down; then lay out crosspieces one at a time. Our grid uses $\frac{5}{8}$- by $1\frac{1}{2}$-inch redwood pieces spaced on 8-inch centers.

    Before assembly, add a dab of waterproof glue where pieces cross. Then nail or screw each intersection. When the finished grid is flipped back over, the fasteners' heads are out of sight.

2   If a simple, standard trellis is all you're after, stop here—you're done! But we decided to add a frame, just for fun. Our frame has 2 by 2 verticals; the top piece was shaped from a 2 by 8. To be on the safe side, wait until you have built the grid before sizing the frame. Countersunk deck screws and glue hold sides to top piece. Wait—don't put the bottom rail on just yet.

3   Grid meets frame. Slide the trellis grid inside the three-sided frame, then snug the bottom 2 by 2 rail up against the grid's bottom edge. The grid is not as thick as the frame; for a nice design touch, line the backs up, leaving a reveal at the front. Screws and glue hold the bottom rail in place; more screws—driven from the outside in—keep the grid in place.

Classic Lath

Traditional garden design often calls for the crisp, milled shapes of what is loosely called "lath"—lumber ranging from about ⅜ to ¾ inch thick and up to 2 inches wide. Redwood and cedar heartwoods are often used for their durability. Pressure-treated lumber works, too, but it can be hard to find in these sizes. If you choose pine or fir, be sure to seal or paint it. Painting is often most easily done before assembly; if you paint after the job is done, consider spray-painting large trellises to save time and energy.

Lath trellises can be freestanding if anchored to stakes or pipe; otherwise, anchor them to a house wall, fence, or roof overhang. If your plants need more grip than lath alone provides, add hardware cloth or nylon netting atop the basic grid.

English garden grids

When it comes to these traditional lath grids, let imagination be your guide. Several possibilities are shown at right. Most versions are surprisingly quick and easy to make.

A gridwork of 1 by 2s is typical; the broad part faces out. For a finished look, use surfaced lumber. Standard grid size is about 6 feet tall by 2 feet wide, but feel free to alter dimensions.

Generally, you build these grids in layers, crisscross fashion, as shown on page 57. Lay down verticals on a flat surface, then place crosspieces on top. Open grid spaces of 6 to 8 inches are the norm, but it's fine to leave some larger openings. Make connections with galvanized nails, screws, or staples; for extra strength, add a dab of waterproof glue to each intersection. The best fastener length is just less than the combined thickness of both parts; for surfaced 1 by 2s, choose about 1¼-inch-long fasteners. If wood tends to split, drill pilot holes first (see page 104).

Circles, arcs, and curlicues can be trickier. If you're planning to paint, they can be fashioned from ¾-inch exterior plywood to match the thickness of surfaced 1 by 2s. Or cut them from wider pieces of 1-by lumber and piece them together as needed. Make a cardboard template, cut it out, and trace it onto the wood (for curve-cutting pointers, see page 102). Fasten these flourishes atop the gridwork as above. If you'd like to "see through" a section with a circle or design, carefully cut out the obstructing inside pieces after everything is assembled.

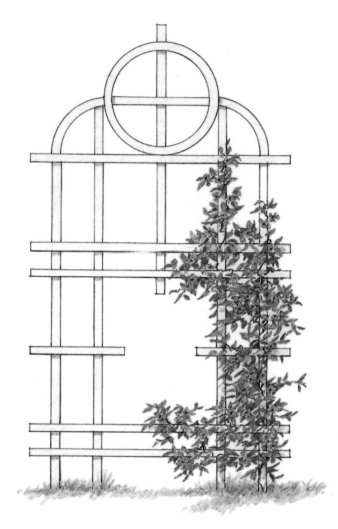

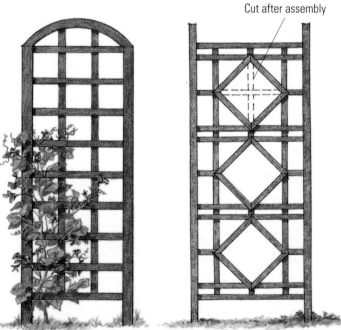

Cut after assembly

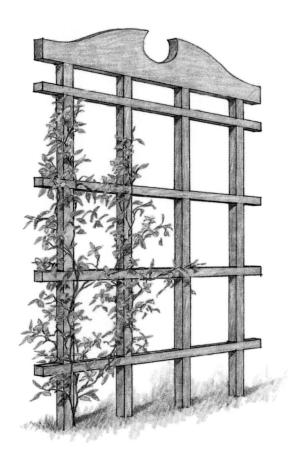

BOLDER GRIDS

For a more graphic, architectural look and a stouter carrying capacity, it's best to scale up to beefier trellis materials like 2 by 2s, or to 2 by 4 verticals and 2 by 2 crosspieces.

You can simply place these layers on top of each other; or, for a sleeker grid joined in a single thickness, cut lap joints where members cross, as shown at right. (For lap-cutting techniques, see pages 103–104.) Be forewarned: For lap joints, you'll probably need power tools to lighten the work load and increase accuracy.

Screws work best for these heavier frames. Before fastening, glue each lap joint with waterproof glue.

The gridwork shown has a decorative top "cap" in a traditional shape; it's cut from a piece of 2 by 8 lumber.

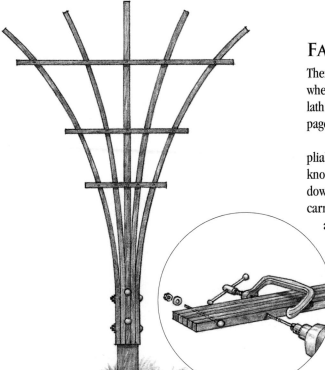

FAMOUS FANS

There are two ways to make popular lathwork fans, depending on whether you want the fan to curve or not. If you don't, use wide lath and follow the basic directions for English grids (facing page), butting together the bottom ends of the verticals.

If you want verticals to arc as shown at left, opt for more pliable 1 by 1 wood strips; choose clear pieces (those without knots) or they may snap. First lay verticals side by side, face down, and clamp them together at the bottom; secure them with carriage bolts, as shown. Then "spread" the fan (you may need an extra pair of hands) and nail on the long top crosspiece. Progressively add remaining crosspieces.

For a freestanding fan, fasten the long center vertical to a stake or reinforcing bar driven into the ground.

GOING RUSTIC

Not all trellises are "straight arrows." The rugged, earthy lines of certain natural materials can be just right for eclectic or cottage-garden landscapes. Twigs, branches, saplings, and vine cuttings are all fair game for rustic designs. If you're citybound, though, the trick is in finding the materials you need. Check with nurseries, talk to landscapers and tree surgeons, or scour empty fields or creek beds.

One of the most useful materials for building garden structures is bamboo: it's lightweight, beautiful, and surprisingly strong, ideal for natural screens and trellises. Although it's been used in Asia for centuries, structural bamboo has only recently become widely available in the United States. Today, you can buy imported bamboo from nurseries and mail-order sources in an array of forms: poles, fences, and water pipes. Also available are specialized tools for working with bamboo.

Wire

RUSTIC TWIG GRIDS

Saplings and prunings make great rustic trellises. Build these with the same crisscrossing verticals and horizontals as more formal lath designs; add diagonals and fan shapes for decoration. Scale them up or down. For a larger, freestanding trellis, look for pieces about 1½ inches thick; for a container-sized version, start with ¾- to 1-inch-thick twigs.

Sometimes such trellises are joined with more formal "lashings," but part of their charm lies in simple construction. Nail twigs together from the back; then, for longer life, wire them together as shown above. Drill pilot holes so the crooked, slippery pieces won't jump around while you nail. If necessary, clamp or tape things together while you work.

GETTING BENT

Part of the fun of working with supple twigs and branches is bending them into decorative shapes. Willow is king here, but other woods, when pliable, work fine too. The key is to use material when it's fresh, preferably within 24 hours after cutting.

To make an arched trellis like those shown at right, you have some options. If you have long lengths of pliable, tapering willow to use, the outside verticals can be laid out as single pieces. For a 6-foot-high by 3-foot-wide arch, you'll need two pieces at least 12 feet long; for a 7- by 2-foot arch, you'll need them a foot or two longer. To be on the safe side, you can overshoot, then trim the bottoms or overlaps to length later. Lay out the crosspieces; then, with a helper on hand, bend the pliable tops until they overlap by several inches and wire them together—quickly. It takes some practice.

If you can't find suitable long material or you just can't win the wrestling match with the pieces, there's another option: build the basic rectangle first, then bend a single piece into an arch and wire it to the verticals on each side.

It's also easy to make a charming arch from multiple strands of very thin saplings or vines bundled together with wire or twine. Wire them to the verticals as outlined above. Just don't expect this arrangement to last forever.

Once the basic structure is intact, you can always add more decorative diagonals and curlicues as you like. Use narrow finish nails for these pieces or simply wire them in place.

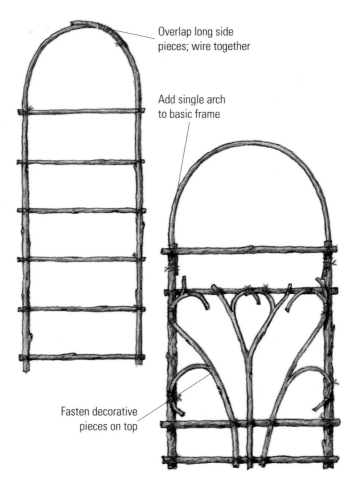

Overlap long side pieces; wire together

Add single arch to basic frame

Fasten decorative pieces on top

CLASSIC BAMBOO GRIDS

Bamboo poles come in roughly ½- to 4-inch diameters and in lengths from 4 to 12 feet. So-called "split" bamboo is not very durable, but it can be useful as horizontal weaving in a stouter whole-pole framework. For large trellis and screen projects, start with 1½-inch poles; smaller grids and fans might use ¾-inch material.

Bind poles where they cross, using either 15-gauge copper wire or precut pieces of galvanized wire (available from bamboo suppliers). Feed the wire through oversized pilot holes as shown in the inset at left, then twist the ends together with a pair of sturdy pliers. Be sure to wear gloves to protect your hands. For a traditional look, cover the wire with black hemp twine: the twine is decorative, while the wire does the work.

Because bamboo poles rot when the ends are buried, it's best to set the trellis on a concrete pad just above soil level. Or slip the pole over a pipe or reinforcing-bar base; the bamboo's solid internodes will keep the pole from sliding down the pipe into the soil. Bamboo also works well when suspended on cedar, redwood, or pressure-treated posts.

Black hemp twine

Pilot hole

Copper wire

PIPE DREAMS

A trip to the hardware store will turn up another family of trellis makings: plumbing pipe. Copper supply pipe, PVC (plastic), and galvanized steel are all suitable—and all come with an array of fittings such as corners, Ts, crosses, and straight couplings, letting you dream up any number of trellis shapes.

Copper is the subtlest looking of the three materials, and it ages to a quiet patina that blends well with plants. Unlike the others, it can be bent. PVC is usually a harsh white in color; it tends to get dirty and fade, but it can be painted. It also tends to sag, so don't plan on using it for long spans. Steel, though a bit pricey, is by far the strongest of these pipes. However, elaborate designs can be hard to pull off because you may need to thread both ends simultaneously. A plumber's trick: Use a union fitting to join difficult straight runs.

You may also come across electrical conduit (EMT). You can even buy it in prebent curves, though most electricians use a conduit bender to custom-shape straight pieces.

Beware: In intense sunlight, metal pipe heats up and may harm plants.

L-fitting

T-fittings

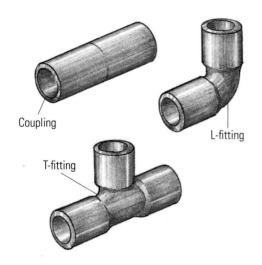

Coupling

L-fitting

T-fitting

A COPPER TRELLIS—AND ARCH?

To make a copper-pipe trellis, lay out a design you like with ½- or ¾-inch supply pipe and matching fittings. Use T-fittings or cross-fittings where pieces "overlap," L-fittings at corners, and couplings to join straight runs. Plumbers "sweat" these joints with watertight solder, but you could opt for a slow-setting epoxy adhesive instead.

If you're more adventurous, try bending copper into an arch with a conduit bender (but be warned—it's tricky). To keep standard pipe from crimping while you bend, fill it with sand first. The design shown above features an arch made with two curved sections joined with a fitting at the top.

Flexible copper tubing, available in thicknesses from ¼ to 1 inch, is the ticket for sharper bends. If you need to join these pieces, consider so-called compression fittings or flare fittings.

CLIMBING THE LADDER

If you'd rather do less work, take advantage of pipe's straight-arrow nature by using it as horizontal "rungs" for a ladder-style trellis like the one shown below. For this design, use matching wood verticals—like 2 by 4s—and drill slightly oversized holes for the electrical conduit or plumbing pipe at about 1-foot intervals. Lock the rungs in place by predrilling pilot holes and driving finish nails in from the back as shown. Copper, PVC, and galvanized pipe all have mating end caps that cover the open ends.

If you prefer, substitute hardwood dowels for the pipes; in this case, it's an easier matter to nail the rungs in place. Seal or paint the dowels first to help preserve them.

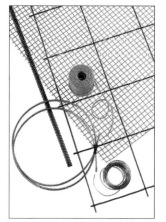

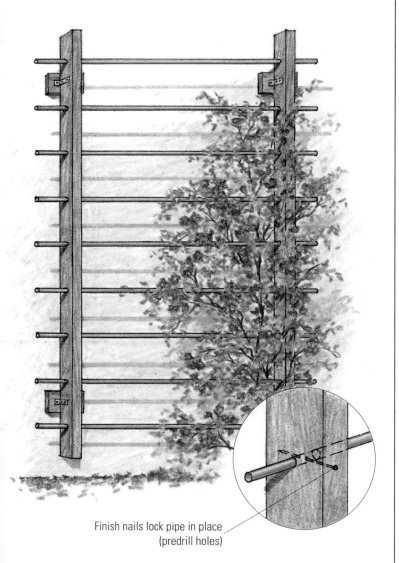

Finish nails lock pipe in place (predrill holes)

GET WIRED

Plumbing pipe isn't the only "found" material at the hardware store. Inventive trellis makers will encounter numerous possibilities among the stacks and bins, especially metals with some structural backbone that can form verticals or horizontals—or shapes incorporating both, in the case of bendable materials.

For starters, you'll find all sorts of loose wires and cables—galvanized, copper, and electrical products. Rope, twine, and thick string are worth a look, too. Hardware cloth, chicken wire, and nylon netting furnish premade "grids" that can be strung atop another frame, a wall, or a fence. Heavier wires include welded steel mesh (typically with 6-inch squares) intended for reinforcing concrete slabs and pathways, as well as the ubiquitous reinforcing bar, which can be bent into all sorts of whimsical shapes (see below and page 7). Unlike the iron and steel bars you might see in commercial trellises, these materials don't require any advanced metalworking skills to work, but you may need wire cutters, a sharp hacksaw, carbide-tipped drill bits, and protective gear such as safety glasses and sturdy gloves.

If you have a penchant for such nonstandard materials, you might also take a stroll through a local steel supplier to discover what other sorts of metal bars, rods, and wire grids might fuel your creative fires. (Look in the Yellow Pages under "Metals" or "Steel Distributors.") And don't rule out salvage yards: items we've seen recycled into trellises include auto parts, fireplace screens, and iron headboards from old beds.

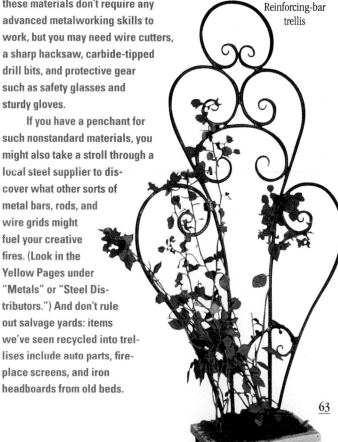

Reinforcing-bar trellis

SHOPPING FOR A TRELLIS

Maybe you don't have time to build your own trellis. Maybe you can't drive a nail to save your life. Or perhaps you want a look that's beyond your design skills or a trellis made from sculpted iron, copper, or architectural steel.

Fortunately, you might find just what you need in one of the new hand-crafted trellises available through garden retailers and mail-order catalogs. Some sources carry an impressive array of trellises—from hand-forged metal types to woven wood models—that are as much a garden focal point as a support for plants.

Purchased trellises are simple to use. Most come ready to install: just push the feet into soil beside a wall or in a planter box, plant a vine, and wrap the stems around the supports (use plant ties when needed). A few need minor assembly, and some wooden ones with feet must be anchored to a wall.

Plant low-growing vines such as black-eyed Susan vine or small clematis on short trellises, taller vines on the others. Rampant growers like silver lace vine and wisteria should be used only on large, sturdy models like the redwood frame pictured on the facing page.

Woven wooden trellises bring a casual touch to the garden, while the architectural wood and metal ones are generally more formal in appearance. Choose a look that fits the surroundings.

For a cottage garden of colorful perennials that overflow their beds, consider a vine trellis or vine arch. These should be attached to a wall or fence.

Sturdier wooden trellises with posts can make freestanding backdrops for roses and perennials. Without posts, they can be anchored to a wall (some have special wall brackets).

Twigs, branches, metal, and lumber: the photos on these two pages show the broad range of shapes, sizes, and styles available among ready-made trellises..

Metal trellises range from whimsical architectural shapes decorated with urns or points of the compass to antique designs custom-fashioned by a blacksmith.

The architectural trellises shown are made of steel. Each is finished slightly differently: some are galvanized steel, others are dark with a hardened oil finish, and still others are covered with lacquer.

The wrought-iron trellis screen (shown at bottom left on this page) is finished in weather-resistant epoxy. Others are fashioned from uncoated copper tubing that weathers to a handsome verdigris.

VEGETABLE MATTERS

Gardeners who want to grow fruits and vegetables but have limited space or poor soil often find that raised beds are the most productive solution to their problems. And to stretch growing space vertically while providing support for such rangy favorites as peas, beans, and some squash, a bedside trellis is made to order.

Though raised beds can be almost any size or shape, there are some guidelines to keep in mind. If the beds are more than 4 feet wide, it will be difficult to reach the middle from either side. When figuring the height of a bed to be built over poor soil, it's a good idea to allow for more than a 1-foot depth of soil.

Should your trellis be permanent, or do you want to tuck it away with the first frost? You'll find both options here.

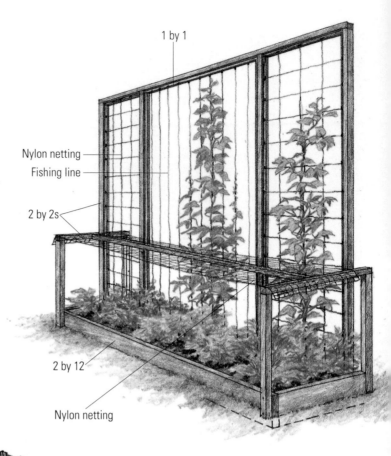

1 by 1

Nylon netting

Fishing line

2 by 2s

2 by 12

Nylon netting

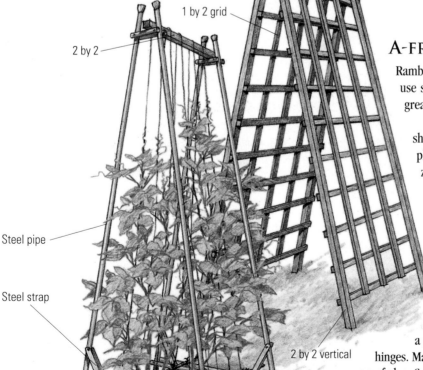

Piano hinge

1 by 2 grid

2 by 2

Steel pipe

Steel strap

2 by 2 vertical

Reinforcing bar

A-FRAMES

Rambunctious beans, melons, and cucumbers can use some support, and a sturdy A-frame trellis is a great way to provide it.

One option is the pipe-frame trellis system shown at far left, made from galvanized steel supply pipes that have been drilled, sprayed with zinc, and bolted together with carriage bolts. Flat steel straps brace the frame's lower end. Lengths of reinforcing bar cross the straps; a 2 by 2 crosses the top. These crosspieces support wire or twine for the vines to climb.

The folding A-frame shown near left is hinged at the top and packs away in winter. It is basically two matching frames built from 2 by 2 verticals and an inner grid of 1 by 2s; join the frames with a galvanized piano hinge or with two sturdy strap hinges. Make connections with nails or screws and waterproof glue. Set the frame directly on the ground atop a planting bed; or spread it to span a raised bed.

A GROW-BOX TRELLIS

The raised box shown on the facing page is made of 2 by 12s anchored in the soil; sheets of ½-inch wire mesh stapled to the box bottom keep out burrowing critters such as gophers. A framework of 2 by 2s over the box supports bird netting, which can be removed as plants mature and become less vulnerable. The framework is 3 feet high, allowing enough room for fairly large plants. A horizontal 2 by 2 beam runs lengthwise over the center of the bed, adding strength to the structure and also holding irrigation tubing. Attached to the beam's underside is a row of microsprayers spaced 2 inches apart. A drip-irrigation line on the surface of the bed supplements the spray system.

A 70-inch-high trellis, made from 2 by 2s and 1 by 1s, runs the length of the box and sits 6 inches in from the edge. String heavy-gauge fishing line up and down in the center section of the trellis to support climbing plants such as beans. For easy assembly, first string the line through 1 by 1s that are predrilled (make the holes 3 inches apart) and then fastened to the inside top and bottom of the trellis.

On the side sections of the trellis, staple nylon netting to the 1 by 1s before attaching them to the inside surfaces of the 2 by 2s. The netting's gridlike structure provides a good hold for plants such as cucumbers.

2 by 2   Bamboo stakes

ZIGZAG TRELLIS FOR BERRIES

Long, rambling blackberry canes tend to grow in chaotic tangles. The sturdy low trellis shown below can help get these unruly vines organized.

The structure is divided into 6-foot lengths. Each ladderlike section features 2 by 3 side pieces with 2-foot 1 by 2 rungs nailed at 1½-foot intervals. Supporting the structure are 2 by 2 posts set 15 inches into the soil (end posts are 2 by 3s). The valleys of the trellis rest 8 inches above ground; the peaks are 2½ feet above ground. First set posts and attach crosspieces that join them; then make ladders and cut end angles to fit together (see page 102).

One berry plant is planted at each low point on the trellis, with canes trained up the structure in both directions except at the ends.

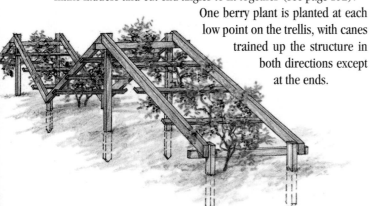

CAGEY IDEAS

Indeterminate tomatoes—rampant, vine-like plants that usually continue to grow until frost kills them—require strong support. A cage trellis offers the easiest means of support; the two shown here are simple to build.

The tepee trellis (above left) is like a stake, but it allows you to grow four plants together. It's made of four 8-foot-long lengths of bamboo lashed together at the top. You can also build it from 1 by 2s, pipe, or tree stakes.

The snazzier square version comes apart for storage at the end of the season. It's built from rough-redwood 2 by 2s and 3-foot-long bamboo stakes (packages of about 18 are available at nurseries).

First, paint the bottom of each 2 by 2 with wood preservative. Then, using a drill with a ¾-inch bit and starting about 30 inches up from the bottom, drill holes through the wood 6 inches apart. Starting about 33 inches up from the bottom on the adjacent side of each post, drill another set of holes 6 inches apart.

To form the cage, set the posts 2½ feet apart in a square and sink them 2 feet into the ground. Set a tomato plant in the middle of the square, then insert two or three levels of bamboo stakes through the posts to steady them. As the plant grows, insert additional stakes.

ON THE MOVE

The trellises on these two pages are designed to be portable. Move them from place to place to catch seasonal sun, then relocate them to a protected area during winter.

The barrel trellis rolls on heavy-duty casters. If you plant the container with annuals such as sweet peas, you can roll it out of view once bloom time ends, replant it with another flowering vine, then trundle it back out when that one is in blossom. The portable screen can back up a planter box, a container, or a dug planting bed; it also serves as a garden divider and helps mask less-than-great views. The wooden obelisk sits in the middle of a lawn or planting bed, serving as both trellis and garden accent.

PORTABLE BARREL TRELLIS

To begin this project, buy an oak half-barrel at a nursery or garden supply store. If you can't find one, use any large, sturdy wooden container at least 2 feet in diameter.

Start by tacking the metal barrel rings in place with roofing nails to keep them from slipping if the barrel dries out and shrinks. Turn the barrel over and bolt the three casters to the bottom. While the barrel is turned over, drill several ¾- to 1-inch-diameter drainage holes in the bottom. To prevent weathering on the outside, brush on several coats of linseed oil. Let the coatings dry. If you like, screw drawer pulls to opposite sides of the barrel.

Then it's time for the trellis. Cut surfaced 2 by 2s into 6½-foot lengths; coat the lower 1½ feet of each post with wood preservative. To make the cross-support, cut an 8-foot 2 by 2 in half. Cut a lap joint in the center of each piece (see pages 103–104 for pointers).

Screw the cross-support to the tops of the four posts with 2½-inch screws so the distance between outside edges of two opposing posts equals the inside diameter of the barrel bottom.

Slip the trellis inside the barrel, spread the legs against the sides, and screw L-brackets to the legs and the barrel bottom.

Cut a 4-foot-square piece of plastic-coated welded wire in half and snip off sharp ends. Slip one piece between two adjacent posts (bending it to fit), about 5 inches down from the top; this gives you enough space at the bottom to cultivate the soil. Line up edges of wire mesh about ½ inch inside the post edges, so cut ends aren't exposed. Staple mesh to the side of each post every 6 inches. Install the second screen on the opposite side. If it doesn't quite fit because it bumps the first screen, offset it slightly, so the bent edges mesh.

Annual vines may need support from netting or string until they reach the wire mesh.

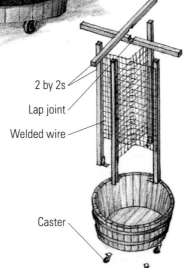

2 by 2s

Lap joint

Welded wire

Caster

A DECORATIVE OBELISK

This project is simple if you have a power saw that cuts compound angles, and pretty tricky if you don't. The basic structure is just a four-sided pyramid made from 1 by 2 redwood legs and crossrungs. It's topped with an overhanging cap cut from a 1 by 8; if you wish, add a decorative post finial or another top ornament.

The obelisk's legs are 6 feet long and are cut at top and bottom with compound 12° angles—that is, they slope from side to side and front to back. A compound miter saw or radial-arm saw can make both these angles at once; otherwise, mark and cut them by hand as best you can. For angle-cutting pointers, see page 102.

To form the obelisk, first assemble two opposing A-frames, each including a pair of legs and three crossrungs. (The end cuts for these rungs are simple—not compound—12° cuts.) Butt the legs at the top and spread them about 2 feet apart below. Make rung-to-leg connections with galvanized finish nails or screws and exterior glue.

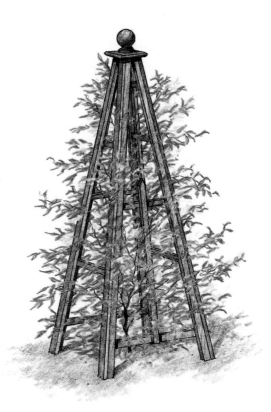

Add a second pair of outside legs to each A-frame, placed at a right angle to the original pair; these new legs form the beginnings of the other two sides. Then bring the opposing A-frames upright and lean them together at the top. Cut and secure an additional pair of rungs on each side as shown, tying the structure together. We also added decorative verticals to both original frames; these spiked pieces are about 3½ feet long.

Let all the wood weather naturally to gray; or, if you like, paint the top ornament a jaunty garden green (or any other color).

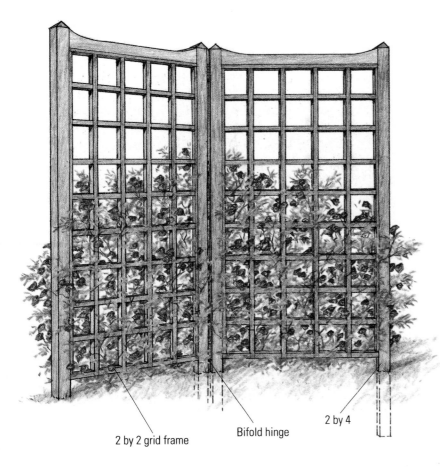

2 by 2 grid frame

Bifold hinge

2 by 4

A LATTICE SCREEN

The trellis shown at left provides both a privacy screen and a growing place for vines—and it can be moved around the garden seasonally as needed.

Build both frames from 2 by 4 surfaced redwood: for each, you'll need two 8-foot-long posts and a 3½-foot-long crosspiece. Woodscrews hold the frames together; three bifold hinges join them at the edges. For a decorative touch, consider shaping the top rails as shown (for techniques, see page 102). You can also round the post edges, post tops, and top rail, but you'll need a router to do it.

Build two lath grids, each about 5 feet tall by 3½ feet wide (measure your frame openings to size them exactly). You can build these with a double layer of 1 by 2s; or, for a more elegant look, join 2 by 2s in a single plane with lap joints (see pages 103–104 for pointers). Attach grids to frames with countersunk screws (see page 104); wood can be left natural or painted to match house or surroundings.

To keep the trellis portable, sink the posts in sand, not concrete. Dig three 2-foot-deep holes (the center hole is widest), fill them with 4 inches of sand, and position the screen in the holes. Then fill in the holes with more sand, packing it in firmly.

FREESTANDING FRAMES

If you're looking for an architectural backdrop, a garden focal point, or a structure to link or define separate garden areas, consider a freestanding trellis. Some of these almost look like arbors—and like arbors, they may require a bit more work to build and install. You'll probably want some extra hands to help lift and position pieces.

Unlike many of their lighter cousins, freestanding frames typically need solid footings of poured concrete. For pointers, see page 107.

HARDWORKING GARDEN TRELLIS

Draped with beans and grapevines, this garden-defining trellis rises from near the center of a long raised bed. The structure combines raised bed, vertical screen for training vines, and decorative horizontal ladder top. You can change the size of the bed to suit the area of your garden.

For the trellis, the 10-foot-long 4 by 4 posts are set 2½ feet into the ground and spaced 4 feet apart on center. Pairs of 2 by 4s flank the post tops and tie them together. The 2½-foot-wide top level is like a horizontal ladder: 1 by 4 rails have 2 by 2 rungs spaced 7 inches apart. The 2 by 2s protrude ½ inch above the top of the rails for a subtly crenellated profile.

The vertical 1 by 1s of the screen mount to 2 by 4s at the top and bottom and to an intermediate 1 by 2 running horizontally between the posts. These horizontal lines are continued by post-wrapping trim pieces, which are butt-joined and nailed in place.

A LATTICE SCREEN TRELLIS

Providing a home for both seasonal plantings and hanging containers, this freestanding lattice screen also separates two garden areas. Prefabricated lattice panels make the structure easier to build; concrete footings hold its hefty framework in place.

To make the screen, you'll need two preassembled 4-by 8-foot lattice panels. Three pairs of 10-foot-long 1 by 4s serve as vertical posts for the sandwich-type frame. Two 9-foot-long 1 by 6s with diagonally cut ends form the horizontal caps. Two pairs of 44-inch-long 1 by 6s are the bottom rails. And three pairs of 2 by 4s—also with ends diagonally cut—form crossbars for hanging plants.

Assemble the screen on the ground, securing it with 1⅝-inch-long drywall screws. Begin with three posts and two bottom rails, laying lattice over the posts and 6 inches below their tops. Fix the remaining posts and rails to the top side of the lattice. Add horizontal caps, then the crossbars. Sink posts 1½ feet deep into concrete.

SINGLE-POLE PLATFORMS

Not all freestanding frames are big and bulky: these two single-pole structures are both handy and relatively easy to install.

Carefully placed, the flower tower (far left) can accent a planting bed, create a garden focal point, and bring fragrance up close. For this rose support, ¾-inch reinforcing bars were welded to a 2-inch steel pipe bolted to a 2½-inch pipe sleeve set in concrete. (You could also through-bolt the horizontal bars with a U-shaped pipe strap.)

The stylized "tree" trellis shown at near left is made from layered 2 by 4 "trunk" and 1 by 4 "branches"; it can display gourd vines, climbing roses, or honeysuckle. For decorative effect, round or chamfer the verticals with a router (see page 105); make contour cuts in the ends of 1 by 4s. Make the trunk any height you like, but don't make the 1 by 4s longer than 1½ feet. Set the trunk in concrete. String wire or rope between a row of "trees" as required to support large plantings.

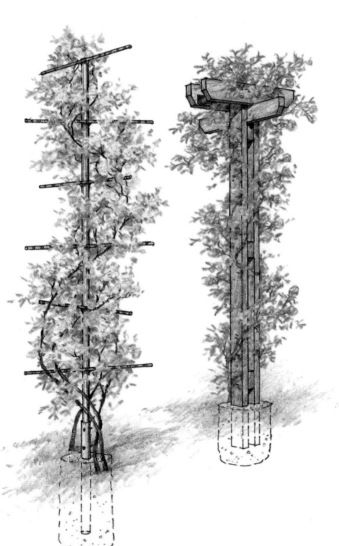

PLANTINGS ON THE WALL

Two-dimensional gardening is a natural for walls and fences, which provide a ready-made backdrop for your efforts. The trick is to combine a pleasing pattern, firm support, and breathing space for plants.

Just about any trellis technique we have shown can serve as a foundation for wall plantings, though lath or wire structures are the most common choices, especially for espalier. The classic espaliering technique was developed by 16th- and 17th-century European gardeners, who succeeded in growing productive fruit trees in confined areas by training the branches into a flat framework. Today, the practice has expanded to include purely ornamental plants, trained both in traditional symmetrical arrangements and in irregular patterns determined by the plant's growth habit.

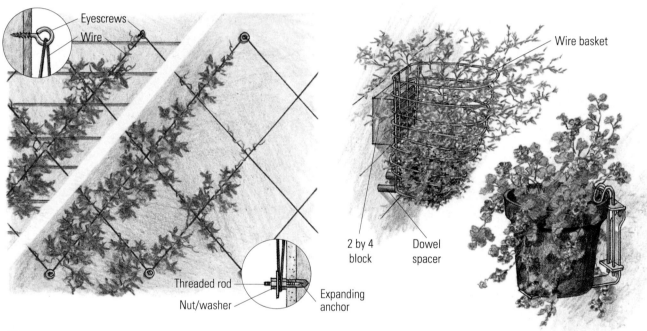

Eyescrews
Wire
Wire basket
Threaded rod
Nut/washer
Expanding anchor
2 by 4 block
Dowel spacer

EASY ESPALIER

For espalier, the basic idea is to direct branches along wires, wood lath, or a wide trellis according to particular two-dimensional patterns like the one shown above left. Any branches that obscure the desired pattern are pruned away. Don't expect the full design to become clear immediately; it will take several years of diligent training and pruning. For an informal espalier, follow the natural shape of the plant, using your sense of artistry as a guide.

For wooden fences or walls, use eyescrews threaded with galvanized wire (12 to 14 gauge). Set wires about 1½ feet apart. Plastic clothesline also makes a strong, discreet framework; attach it to fence or siding as you would wire, using eyescrews.

You can also mount redwood strips, copper pipe, or prefab lattice panels to fence posts or a wall. Use lag screws, galvanized

nails, or U-shaped staples for fastening to wood. Leave some breathing room between trellis and wall; wood spacer blocks, pipes, or metal washers will do the trick.

For masonry walls, choose expanding anchors with screws or lag screws or, as shown above left, threaded rod, nuts, and washers.

Another option is to hang containers with colorful plantings on walls and fences. As shown above right, a 2 by 4 block stapled to the back of each basket allows air circulation and prevents moisture from staining the wall; dowels keep the basket straight. Plan to fasten the block to wall framing, not just siding—baskets full of plants and soil are often heavier than they look. You can also suspend the containers from decorative brackets, but be sure they're rated for the weight.

WINDOW-BOX GARDENING

Seen from outdoors, window boxes provide an accent that can enliven a house's entire facade; seen from inside, they bring color to eye level and provide a visual transition from indoors to out. A trellis like the one shown at right can extend your plantings up, around, and even over the window to soften a less-than-desirable view.

A wall-hung box is heavy when planted, so it must be attached with strong metal brackets. Most building codes require at least a 2-inch-wide air space between box and wall; some may require galvanized-metal flashing behind the box. Be sure that drainage holes aren't too close to the back of the box.

The trellis part is easy. Plan to frame window sides with either flat lath panels or preassembled lattice; or, as shown at right, build matching "wings" to flank the box, then join them with a simple lath roof on top. Anchor them to wood or masonry siding as discussed on the facing page.

To shade a southern exposure or camouflage an unwanted view completely, position an additional lath panel or vertical plant wires a few feet from the window; you might also add lighting from above, under the eave. The plants in the window box will become the focus of a new, entirely private view that shuts out the larger one beyond.

2 by 2 beam 1 by 2 rafters

1 by 2 frame

ABOVE: A tall fence gains an open feel via airy trellis sections on top and a lateral trellis "wing" to the right.

RIGHT: Peach trees form a Belgian fence pattern.

FACELIFTS FOR FENCES

Wooden fences have advantages—they add privacy and mask ugly views. On the down side, they can look blank and boring, and they may create a claustrophobic atmosphere. But most fences do provide handy attachment points for mounted trellises and espalier; and if you're building a new fence, you may be able to combine solid panels with looser sections of trellis or latticework to gain the best of both worlds.

If you're dressing up an existing fence, your trellis verticals—the fence posts—may already be in place. You can also add a trellis and hanging boxes atop the existing structure (but first check limits on fence heights in your area).

If you're designing a fence from scratch, you have other options. Alternating sections of solid boards and lattice panels can alleviate the "prison syndrome" generated by some blank fence designs. Maybe a lattice fence or post-and-rail design and some thick plantings are all you need. Extension wings like those shown on page 12 stretch planting space and help break up a long fence run.

Arbors are by nature somewhat more complex than trellises to lay out and build. Once you understand some basic principles, though, you may find that the job isn't so tough after all.

ARBOR
IDEAS

Whether you call it an arch arbor, overhead, bower, pergola, or gazebo, an arbor is essentially a three-dimensional trellis. Some arbors are intimate; others are overtly architectural. Big or small, they generally share common elements such as uprights, crossbeams, and a roof arch or rafters. We begin this chapter by addressing these components in more detail. We also show you how to build a basic arbor, step by step.

The designs that follow run the gamut of sizes and styles, from gingerbread entry arches through rustic bowers to large-scale overheads. There's even a classic eight-sided gazebo. In many cases, the plans can be scaled up or down. If a material or technique has you baffled, consult "Nuts and Bolts," beginning on page 95, for an explanation.

Along the way, you'll also find feature boxes detailing such add-ons as benches, screens, and roofing—the amenities that help turn a basic arbor into a cozy outdoor room.

Climbing roses are a good match for the clean lines of this classic, white-painted arch arbor.

ARBOR-BUILDING BASICS

In its simplest form, an arbor is a three-dimensional trellis, with two parallel trellis sides and a third, horizontal trellis as a roof. Some arbors are lightweights; others are heavier structures, designed to house both plants and people. The bigger the arbor, the more carefully you'll need to design its components. Here's an overview of the planning process.

DESIGN OPTIONS

The key to arbor construction is to think of a crisscross or stacking principle, with each new layer placed perpendicular to the one below it. Keep in mind that, although you build an arbor from the ground up, you should design it from the top down: the kind of roof you choose will influence the size and spacing of the support members below.

Whether freestanding or attached to a building, an arbor is held up by a series of posts or columns. These support horizontal beams, which in turn support rafters. For added strength, the structure can be braced where the posts meet the beams. You have numerous options for combining posts, beams, and rafters; the choices you make will largely determine your arbor's appearance. In a house-attached overhead, a ledger (see page 87) takes the place of one beam, and the rafters are connected directly to it.

The rafters can be left bare; or they can be covered with more lumber or with lath, lattice, poles, woven reeds and wood, bamboo, tree stakes, or grape stakes. Such "open" arbors don't collect much rain or snow, so they must support only the weight of the materials themselves plus that of any plants growing on them. For sizing guidelines, see "Calculating Spans," page 78.

As you plan, check with your local building department for information on regulations affecting your project's size, design, and construction. In many communities, you will have to meet building codes and obtain a permit before you begin work.

Arbor-building Basics continues >

Rafters sit atop beams

Posts are 4 by 4 lumber or larger; metal anchors secure posts to piers

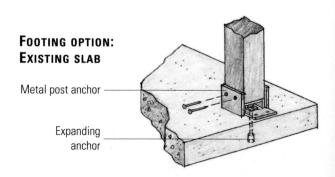

FOOTING OPTION: EXISTING SLAB

Metal post anchor

Expanding anchor

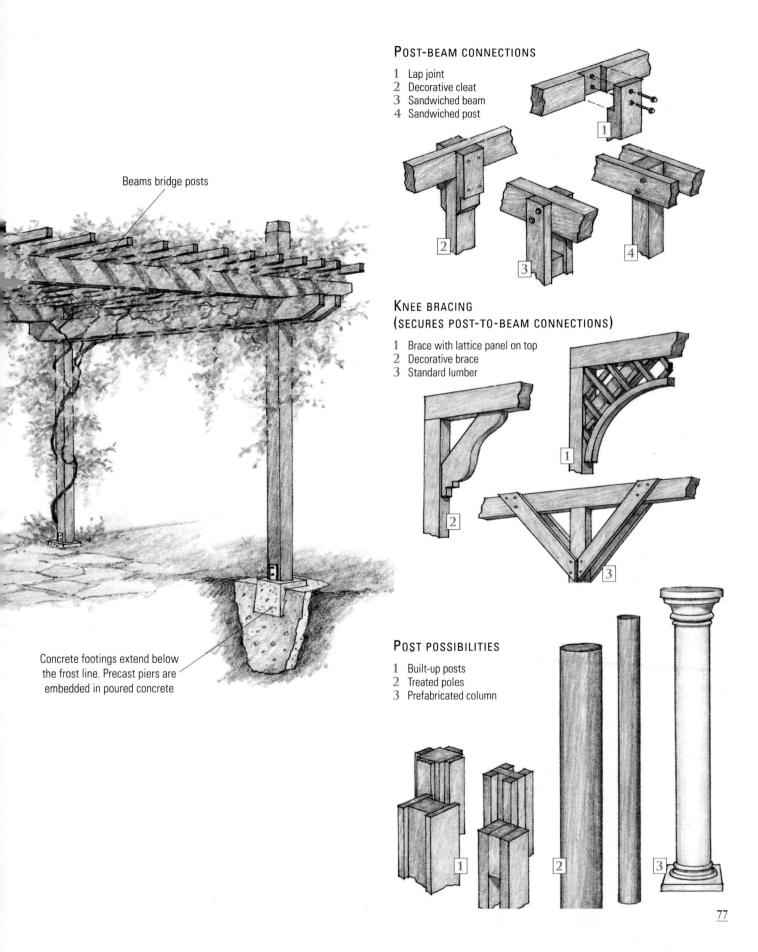

Beams bridge posts

Concrete footings extend below the frost line. Precast piers are embedded in poured concrete

POST-BEAM CONNECTIONS

1 Lap joint
2 Decorative cleat
3 Sandwiched beam
4 Sandwiched post

KNEE BRACING
(SECURES POST-TO-BEAM CONNECTIONS)

1 Brace with lattice panel on top
2 Decorative brace
3 Standard lumber

POST POSSIBILITIES

1 Built-up posts
2 Treated poles
3 Prefabricated column

MATERIALS

Most arbors are built from standard dimension lumber (see pages 96–97). You can use 4 by 4 posts for most overheads; exceptions are very tall (over 12-foot) structures. The size of beams and rafters depends on the unsupported distances they must span. As shown on page 77, you can often substitute two or more pieces of 2-by lumber for a single 4-by post or beam.

To maximize the life of an arbor, it's best to use either pressure-treated lumber or naturally decay-resistant materials such as redwood or cedar heartwood. (You'll probably want to paint pressure-treated lumber to mask its greenish color.)

Choose sturdy nails, screws, lag screws, and bolts for arbor projects. Prefabricated metal framing connectors can help secure joints between structural members. For a closer look at all these fasteners, see pages 98–99.

WHAT'S INVOLVED?

Building most arbors is within the reach of a do-it-yourselfer. Lightweight arch designs are really no tougher to put together than many trellises. Tools are basic: you'll need a saw, a tape measure, a hammer, a carpenter's level, and probably a power drill with bits. For details, see pages 100–101.

Even most large-scale overheads are assembled with basic butt joints. If you'll need to raise heavy beams, however, make sure you have a helper or two.

Angles, bevels, and trim cuts are more easily done with power saws. (For tips and techniques, see pages 102–103). A portable router and bit can make short work of decorative details like grooves, chamfers, and rounded edges—but many designs, especially those on the rustic side, look fine without these touches.

CALCULATING SPANS

The number, size, and spacing of an arbor's beams, rafters, and posts are determined by the loads they must carry. Open overheads don't collect much rain or snow, so they must support only the weight of the materials themselves. This generally works out to about 5 pounds per square foot (psf).

The tables below give maximum recommended beam and rafter spans for a standard overhead, such as the one discussed on pages 76–77. The spans are based on a load of 5 pounds psf and No. 2 and Better lumber. Keep in mind that smaller, simpler structures such as arch arbors, frames, and twig tunnels won't require this level of "engineering."

The main restriction on your overhead's design will be the placement of the posts, which is critical both for the look of the arbor and for directing traffic flow below. You can use 4 by 4 posts for most overheads. Exceptions are very tall structures—those over 12 feet.

Once you have decided on the positioning of the posts, you can determine the size of the beams. The distance between posts is the distance your beams must span. That, plus the spacing between parallel beams, determines the size of lumber you'll need. Table 1 lists these beam sizes. Remember that you can substitute two 2-by beams for one 4-by beam, though it's generally a good idea to jump up one size (for example, use two 2 by 10s instead of one 4 by 8).The beam spacing will determine the rafter span. Working from this number, use Table 2 to figure the size and spacing of the rafters (rafter spacing will be limited by the cover materials you choose, although most will allow at least 2-foot spacings).

TABLE 1: MAXIMUM RECOMMENDED BEAM SPANS

BEAM SIZE	MAXIMUM SPACING BETWEEN BEAMS*	
	12'	16'
2 x 10	10'	16'
2 x 12	14'	12'
3 x 6	8'	6'
3 x 8	10'	8'
3 x 10	12'	10'
3 x 12	16'	14'
4 x 4	6'	4'
4 x 6	8'	6'
4 x 8	12'	10'
4 x 10	14'	12'
4 x 12	18'	16'

*or between beam and ledger

TABLE 2: MAXIMUM RECOMMENDED RAFTER SPANS

RAFTER SIZE	MAXIMUM RAFTER SPACING		
	12"	16"	24"
2 x 4	10'	9'	8'
2 x 6	16'	14'	12'
2 x 8	20'	18'	16'

ASSEMBLING A BASIC ARBOR

1 This flat-roofed arbor begins with two 4 by 4 posts and two sandwiched pairs of 2 by 4 crossrungs. You can attach the rungs on the ground, as we did here, then anchor the posts carefully in concrete while plumbing and leveling crossrungs. Or you can secure posts first, cut their tops level, and then add the 2 by 4s aloft.

With either approach, attach pairs to posts with two carriage bolts. Clamp the assembly together first; then drill all the way through all three thicknesses. A larger countersink hole (see page 104) helps conceal each bolt's washer and nut. Use a ratchet-and-socket set to drive the nuts below the surface.

2 Now we're aloft on a ladder, positioning twin 2 by 6 beams atop the paired crossrungs. Secure these pieces with framing connectors from behind, or by toenailing. We've added some decorative touches to the beams, including angled ends and a pair of notches that lock into the crossrungs, but you could opt for simple, straight beams that sit on top.

3 We're in the home stretch. With posts aloft and beams secured, complete the arbor with an open roof of evenly spaced 2 by 2 rafters that bridge both beams. Simply nail these pieces in place from the top down; if wood splits, drill pilot holes first (see page 104).

ELEGANT ENTRIES

Why not frame a front entry, a side gate, or a secluded garden path in romance and leafy style? We show three basic variations on the entry arbor theme: arched, peaked, and flat. Each category offers almost infinite options: by subtly varying the side walls, post-to-beam connections, and roofing, you can give a structure quite a different look.

Each arbor is anchored by four sturdy posts, bridged by beams, and roofed with crosspieces that form a trellis and tie the components together. Side walls are ornamental lattice or lath gridwork.

These arbors should be a minimum of 6 feet 8 inches tall (the height of an interior door) and at least 4 feet wide to allow easy movement; most are taller and wider. For an extra-wide span, beef up beams and brace them to the posts (for span guidelines, see page 78). Plan to anchor posts to concrete footings.

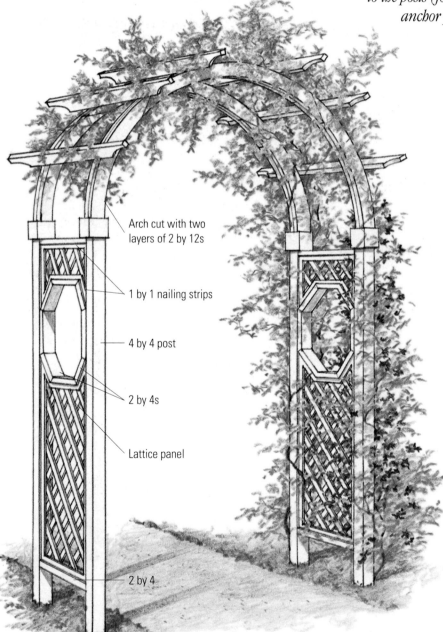

Arch cut with two layers of 2 by 12s

1 by 1 nailing strips

4 by 4 post

2 by 4s

Lattice panel

2 by 4

A FORMAL ENTRY ARCH

This arching entry arbor invites guests to the front door. The arch is built from a double thickness of 2 by 12s cut into arcs and nailed together; joints are staggered between front and back sections. The resulting arch is sanded, caulked, and painted to hide joints. For curve-cutting pointers, see page 102.

Posts are 4 by 4s; they're bridged by 2 by 4s at top and bottom. These side frames are 6 feet tall by 2 feet wide; the opening between them is 6 feet 7 inches. Alter dimensions to fit the scale of your path and landscape.

For sides, prefabricated lattice panels are cut to fit the framing; 1 by 1 nailing strips on both sides hold them in place. The octagonal cutouts are framed with 2 by 4s mitered at 22½° angles; for a simpler structure, just leave them out. Or substitute lathwork grids (see page 58) for the lattice panels.

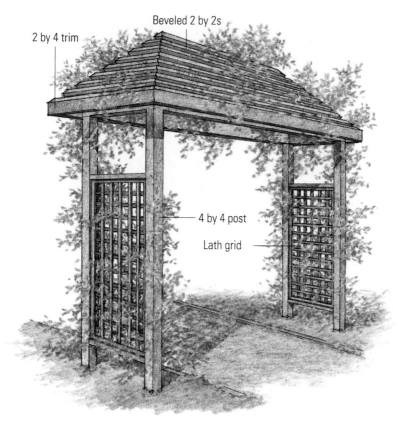

Beveled 2 by 2s

2 by 4 trim

4 by 4 post

Lath grid

PEAKS AND VALLEYS

Shown at left are two variations on the classic arch arbor. The first has a traditional pitched roof, the second a sleeker flat roof. Both roofs are open, giving them a less dominating look and providing a toehold for plants.

The peak is framed with traditional angled rafters; they're lengths of 2 by 4 lumber. The roof slats are fashioned from equally spaced 2 by 2s, beveled on their outside edges to follow the roof's slope. Corner rafters, which help form the end "hips," are beveled on top to allow the 2 by 2s to sit flat. On the sides, lath grids (much like those shown on page 58) sit inside 4 by 4 posts. For more on roof framing, see *Sunset's Basic Carpentry.* Or, if this particular job isn't your specialty, you can substitute simpler beam-and-rafter construction, as shown on pages 76–77.

The flat-roofed entry arbor is more straightforward to build, though you'll need power tools to cut the optional decorative grooves. The 14-foot-long structure might span a path winding through a side courtyard (between garage and house, for example).

Layers of wood with faceted cuts contribute details to the arbor. Supporting the structure are two pairs of pressure-treated 4 by 4s partially masked by added 1 by 4s and notched 2 by 4s. Capitals of 4 by 6s with rabbeted edges support 2 by 6s that span the posts. The top layer has pairs of 2 by 3s with notched ends.

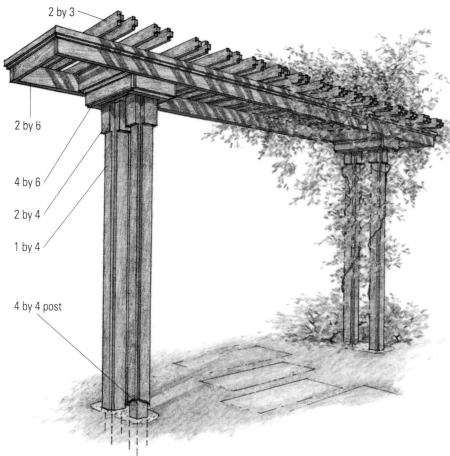

2 by 3

2 by 6

4 by 6

2 by 4

1 by 4

4 by 4 post

ARCHED EXPRESSIONS

Most large arbors are built according to the stacking principles shown on pages 76–77. Some more modest, more decorative structures, however, are intended primarily as three-dimensional trellises—and that's the key to their design and construction.

Almost any of the materials featured in the trellis projects on pages 58–73 can be used for a lightweight arch arbor. The idea is simply to design and build two walls and a roof—three trellises, if you like—and brace them together. Or build multiple arched trellises, line them up, and tie them together to form a deeper "tunnel." We show several rustic options here, but materials like lath, bamboo, plumbing pipe, and reinforcing bar work just as well.

Like the entry arbors on pages 80–81, these lightweight arches can be built wide enough to frame a pathway; most, however, simply form freestanding ornamental backdrops in the landscape. You probably won't need to set these in concrete footings; instead, anchor them like trellises (see page 104) by fastening them to metal pipes, reinforcing bar, or stakes that are, in turn, driven into the ground.

LEAFY LADDERS

The sapling arbor shown above is basically just three ladder trellises—two parallel walls and a roof bridging them. Build the trellises as outlined on page 60; fasten the pieces together with nails, with wire or twine, or with a combination of both. You'll need to add diagonal braces, as shown, to lock the arbor together—a step that also allows you to create a more interesting arch shape without bending anything. Once the basic structure is intact, nail on smaller, more decorative pieces to your heart's content.

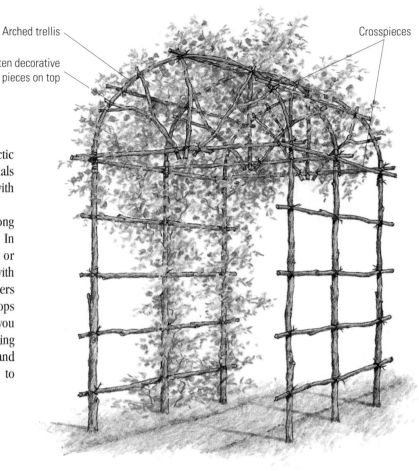

Arched trellis

Fasten decorative pieces on top

Crosspieces

TWIGS AND VINES

Rustic arch arbors are favorites for country or eclectic gardens: build them from simple "found" materials like cuttings or woven vines, then blanket them with roses or other colorful climbers.

The bentwood arches shown at right have a strong resemblance to the trellises illustrated on page 61. In fact, these tunnel structures are simply two, three, or more hoops made in like dimensions, then joined with crosspieces at the side and along the tops. Beginners may have a hard time forming three consistent hoops with a succession of single, bending side pieces; if you prefer, build this tunnel "sideways" by first erecting rectangular walls, then bridging them front, back, and center with supple prunings or woven vines. Plan to link the arches across their width as shown.

EASY-TO-BUILD ARCH ARBOR

You don't have to be a crackerjack carpenter to build an impressive arbor like the one shown at left. Starting with four ready-made arch arbors, you should be able to assemble the structure in a day.

The homeowner-designers bought the redwood arches at a nursery. Each has a pair of frames spaced 2 feet apart, with an opening wide enough to bridge a 4-foot-wide path. After painting the arches, the owners spaced them evenly along the house wall, set the legs in concrete, and fastened the frames to the wall on one side with barbed nails.

They then linked the four arches with 2 by 2s, butted end to end and nailed to the top seven 1 by 2s spanning the top of each arch. Connections were made with screws running up through the 1 by 2s and into the 2 by 2s. The leaves and delicate pink blooms of climbing roses spill over the curving tops of the arches, brush against the windows of the house, and dangle into the tunnel-like passage below.

BOWER BASICS

Nestled in lush surroundings, the retreats shown here are not only handy frames for plants, but also quiet spots for reading, relaxation, moon-watching, and contemplation—escapes from the hurried pace of everyday life.

In its traditional form, a bower is a garden shelter formed by vines or tree boughs twined together (for ideas, see page 93). Today, the distinction between bower and arbor has become blurred—but most bowers have more the shape of a simple house, sometimes with a peaked roof, and are intended as a cool place to sit and relax. They may include either built-in seating or movable benches or chairs.

The sides and back can be open or filled in with trellis materials such as lattice, lath, or wires for vines. Consider a trickling wall fountain or spill fountain nearby. If you'll be visiting at night, you may wish to add subtle but functional outdoor lighting, such as downlights inside the roof structure, uplights near the base, or decorative, softly glowing strip lights.

2 by 4 rafter, notched atop beams

4 by 6 beams

Lattice panel

4 by 4 posts

¾" exterior plywood

2 by 2 nailing strips

2 by 6

2 by 8

A GARDEN HIDEAWAY

A comfortable garden bench forms the centerpiece of this charming retreat; vines climb up and over the lattice gridwork. Structurally speaking, it's sort of like a carport—but it houses plants and people rather than hulking vehicles.

The basic bower is 12 feet long by 3 feet deep; it's made from prefabricated lattice panels mounted on 4 by 4 posts. The overhanging rafters are 2 by 4s spaced on 13-inch centers. The posts in each group are spaced 2 feet apart laterally and 3 feet front-to-back; the roof overhangs 1½ feet. The center bench is 8 feet long and is made from 2 by 8 framing and 2 by 6 seat slats.

Solid front and back sections are ¾-inch exterior plywood. A wall fountain accents the plywood panel behind the bench. The entire structure is painted white to give it a crisp, traditional look and to blend plywood, lattice, and lumber.

30° end cuts

2 by 4 top plate

2 by 4 rafter

4 by 4 post

1 by 2 lath

2 by 6 benches

Brace

A RUSTIC REDWOOD RETREAT

This gambrel-roofed "house" is framed with sturdy rough red-wood that has been assembled in simple, rustic fashion; it will weather to a quiet, understated gray. The plants, not the bower, provide both privacy and decorative color.

The only trick to building such a peaked structure is making the angled cuts that join the rafters. We've shown a gambrel shape, but you might prefer a straightforward peak or flat roofline. The key to compound angles is to build the roof frame first—on the ground—then fine-tune the post spacings to match. Feel free to fill in sides and back with trelliswork, or to add additional roofing materials.

If your structure is at least 4 feet deep (like the one shown), you'll have room for side benches; build frame, back-rest, and bracing as shown.

SITTING PRETTY

Though commercial benches and other garden seating are readily available, designing and building your own allows you to blend the seating with your arbor's design and, in many cases, to take advantage of posts or other support members for partial support.

When designing a bench, keep in mind that, for maximum comfort, it should be 15 to 18 inches high—equal to or slightly lower than the approximate height of most chairs. If you plan to use a thick mat or cushion, make the seat lower to allow for it.

There is no set guide for depth. A bench only 1 foot deep, though common, is more of a perch than a place to relax. A depth of 15 to 18 inches is comfortable, but you can make the seat even deeper for lounging.

Legs or supporting members should be sturdy enough for solid support but in scale with the rest of the bench. If the legs are made from 4 by 4s or a material of similar strength, space them 3 to 5 feet apart. If you're using a lighter material or if the lumber for the top of the seat needs additional support to prevent it from sagging, place the legs closer together. Be sure to allow for a kickspace beneath the bench; seating that doesn't let you tuck your feet under can be very uncomfortable.

For strength, use 2-by lumber for bench seats. A single wide plank, such as a 2 by 12, may look stronger than two 2 by 6s or three 2 by 4s, but it will have a greater tendency to warp or split. Always use surfaced lumber for seating. Prebore holes for screws and bolts, and countersink them so the heads don't extend above the surface to skewer the unwary. Sand or plane any exposed surfaces; smooth and round off edges.

An entry arbor with built-in benches

GROWING ATTACHED

Not all arbors can stand alone. Some take advantage of walls or decks to gain both a structural "leg up" and a look that blends with the house or with other outdoor structures.

A house-attached overhead is built much like the freestanding arbor discussed on pages 76–77, but a house wall, garden wall, or other structure takes the place of two of the posts and one of the principal beams. A so-called ledger, usually made from 2-by material, is securely mounted to the wall at beam height; rafters sit atop the ledger or are attached to its face via metal joist hangers (see page 99). Plan to fasten the ledger to wall studs or a second floor's framing inside the wall, not just to wood siding or stucco. If you cantilever a lightweight arbor on sturdy decorative brackets (as shown on the facing page), you may not need posts at all.

A deck-attached arbor such as the corner unit shown at right is a backyard destination, a decorative backdrop, and a privacy screen or windbreak all rolled into one. You build the structure as you would any other overhead, but instead of anchoring posts in concrete footings, you bolt them securely to the deck's substructure, then cut surface decking to fit around the posts.

DECK-ATTACHED CORNER ARBOR

Elegantly framing the corner of a deck, this L-shaped arbor offers comfortable seating for people as well as ample footholds for climbing plants. Its charm is the result of interesting detailing and careful workmanship—evidenced in its bandsawed knee braces and decorative bench.

The 4 by 4 posts hold 4 by 6 beams and 2 by 4 rafters aloft. The benches are framed with 2 by 4s and surfaced with 2 by 6s. Cushions purchased at an outdoor furniture store could soften the seats. To brighten the space at night, you might secure outdoor light fixtures to the rafters.

If you're building deck and arbor at the same time, the deck posts can extend up to serve the arbor, too; otherwise, bolt the arbor's posts to the deck substructure as shown in the inset below left. Cut the deck's surface boards to fit around the posts.

Overhead post

Machine bolts

Joist

Deck post

Deck beam

4 by 4 posts
(anchor to deck framing)

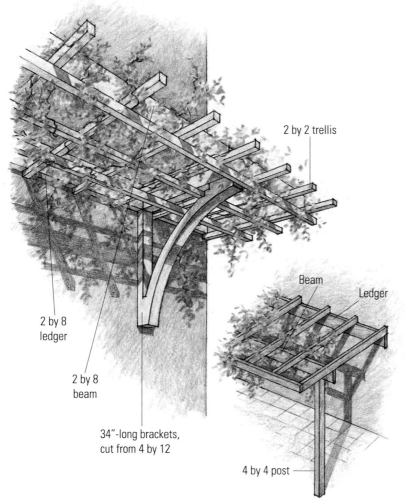

2 by 2 trellis

2 by 8 ledger

2 by 8 beam

34"-long brackets, cut from 4 by 12

Beam

Ledger

4 by 4 post

HOUSE-ATTACHED ARBOR ROOF

The graceful arbor shown above left defines and unifies the rear of a narrow house. To give the overhead a lighter look, a trellis grid of 2 by 2s floats on the underside of the supporting framework. The structure extends from the house wall on curving, 34-inch-long brackets cut from 4 by 12s. You'd need a bandsaw to cut these shapes; as a simpler alternative, consider straight brackets made from wood or steel.

The structure is bolted to the house wall via a 2 by 8 ledger. A matching 2 by 8 beam sits atop the brackets extending from the house.

For a simpler, larger, more traditional structure, install the ledger, but use 4 by 4 posts to support the outside beam, as shown above right. These posts should be anchored to strong concrete footings.

Fasten ledgers to wood siding with lag screws (see page 98). For masonry walls, choose expanding anchors instead. To prevent rot, space a ledger away from a wooden wall with blocks or washers, or install metal flashing atop it.

Formal trellis screen

WALLS AND CEILINGS

Overheads become outdoor rooms with the addition of walls and ceilings—or, more precisely, screens and roofing.

For "screens," read "trellises." Used as outdoor walls, these not only provide barriers to block objectionable views, add privacy, or moderate or filter winds, but also give vines and climbing roses a running start towards the arbor's rafters. The arbor's posts serve as a wall frame: nailing strips or a grooved lumber strip are fastened vertically to them, serving to center the screen in place.

Prefabricated lattice panels are easiest to add. Lath grids, especially those constructed with interlocking lap joints (see pages 103–104), are more stylish, looking like divided windows. Woven reeds, woven woods, and split bamboo will all filter breezes, but they aren't very durable; solid bamboo (page 61) or prefabricated bamboo screens are better bets.

Roof covers are applied atop the overhead structure of beams and rafters. Open designs block the sun, frame a view, and create a feeling of enclosure, but don't keep out hard rain or snow. They're also plant-friendly.

Solid roofs shelter the area below from rain and snow. Materials you can install yourself include asphalt shingles, wood shingles and shakes, siding, asphalt roll roofing, and aluminum shingles. These roofs must slope a minimum of ¼ inch per foot to allow for runoff.

Tree-stake roofing

Plastic or glass is another option; both materials can maximize light, view, and shelter. If improperly designed, however, a plastic or glass roof can act as a heat trap or create a condensation and drip problem.

Because of the weight of solid roofing materials and the snow they may collect, solid roof designs are best reviewed by a professional.

ARCHITECTURAL OVERHEADS

A good overhead arbor bridges interior and exterior spaces, taking its cue from your home's architectural style. On a hot day, it can transform a scorching patio or deck into a shady refuge; in inclement weather, it can block wind and rain, letting you entertain and relax outdoors when you'd otherwise be stuck inside. Leafy deciduous vines provide shade in summer; after leaves drop in autumn, more light and heat (as well as rain or snow) will come through.

Design your overhead's frame according to the stacking principle outlined on pages 76–77. These outdoor rooms should match the ones indoors in height—make them at least 7½ feet tall. Concrete footings secure the posts to bare ground. To connect them to a patio slab, use metal post anchors; to connect to a deck, use bolts.

Even if you're pounding the nails yourself, you may wish to have an architect or designer lay out the structure to make sure it harmonizes with your house. And always check local codes and zoning ordinances that may affect your plans.

Lattice panel

2 by 6

4 by 4 post

ALL THE TRIMMINGS

To spruce up the basic overhead, you have a number of design options for posts, beams, and rafters. Several are shown on pages 76–77. You might also opt for some trimwork, as shown here; these treatments look snazzy, and most are easy to add.

When it comes to posts and beams, you have two trim choices: applied trim and shaping. To give a plain, bland post additional shape, you can apply 1-by or 2-by lumber to it with finish nails. A column effect can be supplied by boxed, mitered trim boards at bottom, top, or center.

You could also shape bevels in the ends of posts or beams, or cut decorative grooves with a power saw before assembly. Or make chamfers, grooves, or rounded edges with a portable router.

Decoratively cut rafter ends (like those shown at right) let you express your creativity and give the arbor roof a distinctive style. You'll see many examples of decorative rafter-tail treatments throughout this book. Though you can make do with a coping saw, it's best to use power tools— either a bandsaw or portable saber saw—for most of these cuts.

Applied post trim

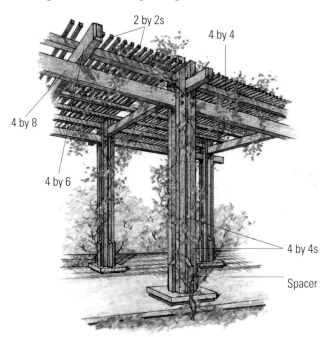

2 by 4s

3 by 3s

2 by 8s

2 by 2s

4 by 4

4 by 8

4 by 6

4 by 4s

Spacer

AN ARBOR BUILT FROM TWOS

One would do, but two are better: that's the idea behind the inviting garden arbor shown at left. Doubling up lumber serves the dual purpose of strengthening the structure and giving it a hand-crafted yet stylish look.

All the wood is standard dimension lumber, though some of it has been artfully disguised. For example, each of the 2-foot-wide corner "columns" is composed of a pair of 4 by 4 posts sandwiched between pairs of 2 by 6s and bridged by lattice panels.

The columns support four layers of lumber, also placed in pairs. The first two layers are 2 by 8s; the top two are 3 by 3s and 2 by 4s. The tapering 2 by 8s that make up the second layer add a woodworking flourish beneath the mantle of sprawling vines.

Built-in planters and a bench bridge two sides of the arbor. The bench is attached to the planters, which in turn are bolted to corner posts, further strengthening the structure.

CRISSCROSS

The stacking principle shown above serves as a very visible design motif: uprights made from four interlocked timbers solidly support a massive overhead trellis.

Each weighty vertical sits atop its own concrete pad footing and is made from four 4 by 4 posts that are held apart at the bottom with decorative, angle-cut 4-by spacers. The gap allows the sandwiched, crisscross motif above—an ascending stack of 4 by 8 and 4 by 6 beams with 4 by 4 rafters. Connections are drilled and secured with sturdy bolts. The top layer of closely spaced 2 by 2s spans the rafters. Beam ends are chamfered (beveled) where they overhang the overhead.

Semitransparent stain protects the wood without obscuring its rough-sawn texture.

Decorative rafter tails

THE PERFECT PERGOLA

What exactly is a pergola? It's simply an arbor laid out colonnade fashion—with opposite rows of equally spaced posts—and draped with climbing plants to form a long, shady tunnel. Classic pergola dimensions follow the 8-foot plan: the structure is 8 feet wide and at least 8 feet tall, and the posts in each row are set 8 feet apart. But feel free to alter the spacing to suit your scale.

A pergola's posts set the style. Though most designs are on the rustic side, posts run the gamut from gnarly timbers and poles, to squared-off dimension lumber with decorative trim, to more elegant, architectural columns of masonry or steel. Longitudinal beams run the length of the pergola from pole to pole; crosspieces connect the rows. Lumber, lath, stakes, or wire form the roof; spacings are determined by what you're planting and how much shade you want.

A GRAPE FACTORY

The perfect grape arbor is a high-volume fruit factory as well as a shady refuge in hot weather. The pergola pictured here provides both plentiful shade and an ample crop of fruit. It's made from eight 9-foot-long, pressure-treated 4 by 6 posts. Each post is anchored in a 1½-foot-deep concrete footing. The posts are set 6 feet apart in two parallel rows, with 12 feet between rows. Four 2 by 10 tie beams connect the rows, while the four posts in each row are connected by 4 by 4s.

On each side of the arbor, strands of heavy-gauge wire are strung horizontally through the 4 by 6s. The vines clamber along these horizontally. Wire also runs at 2-foot intervals across the top of the pergola, letting the vines climb over the structure.

When the grapes ripen, the clusters hang down from the top and sides of the structure, where they're easy to see and pick. To protect the fruit, the entire arbor can be covered with bird netting

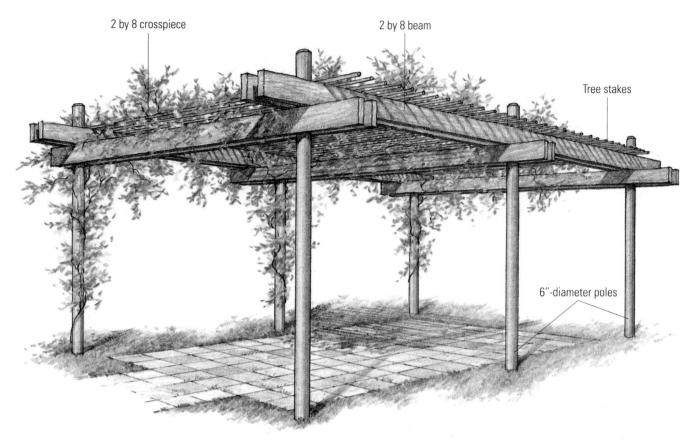

2 by 8 crosspiece

2 by 8 beam

Tree stakes

6"-diameter poles

POLE PERGOLA

This version of the classic pergola (above) has a slightly more rustic appearance than dimension lumber alone can provide. Pressure-treated, 6-inch-diameter poles are spaced 8 feet apart down the rows and 8 feet across in matching sets. Pairs of 2 by 8 crosspieces sandwich each set of poles; they're held in place with bolts. Longitudinal beams go above; they too are bolted in place. For a rustic look, use rough lumber; for a slightly more finished appearance, choose surfaced, pressure-treated dimension lumber (see page 97). Plan to paint or stain the poles. Other lumber can be sealed or, in the case of redwood or cedar, left to go gray naturally.

The top trellis is made from overhanging lengths of tree stakes for a rustic look that matches the poles. You could also make the trellis from 2 by 2s or simply string wire across the pergola's top to support vines. If you'd like the trellis to run lengthwise instead, put the longitudinal beams on first, then the crossbraces, and finally the long roof slats.

If poles and tree stakes aren't your thing, consider the more uniform version of this project shown at right. This structure combines 4 by 4 posts with 4 by 6 beams and crossbraces, plus evenly spaced 2 by 2 roof slats on top. For extra strength, plan to make post-beam-crosspiece connections using sturdy metal framing connectors (see page 99); or add knee braces (see page 77).

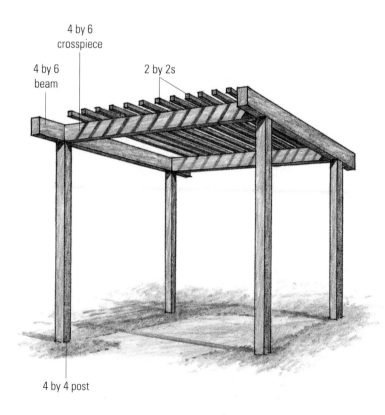

4 by 6 crosspiece

4 by 6 beam

2 by 2s

4 by 4 post

Gazebo Magic

Reminiscent of country bandstands in small-town parks, gazebos can be romantic garden hideaways. The traditional gazebo is a freestanding version of an overhead, with either six or eight sides and sloping rafters that join in a central hub at the roof peak. Often the sides are partially enclosed with lath, lattice, or even metal grillwork; climbing vines may adorn them.

Contemporary gazebos frequently depart from the old-fashioned Victorian style. Construction can be substantial—with hefty corner columns and stacked beams—or light, with little more than four posts connected by pairs of 2 by 6s. The design may be enhanced by features such as path lighting or downlights, built-in benches or swings, window boxes, fountains, or spas.

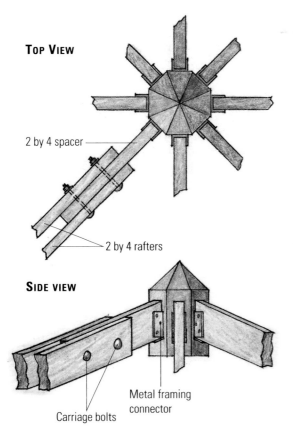

TOP VIEW

2 by 4 spacer

2 by 4 rafters

SIDE VIEW

Carriage bolts

Metal framing connector

SCREENED GAZEBO

On this gazebo, screens of closely spaced boards provide protection from sun and wind as well as footholds for climbing plants.

You can set the posts in concrete directly in the ground, attach them to post anchors set in concrete footings, or fasten them to the substructure of a deck. Attach 2 by 4 crosspieces except where you want access.

You can fashion the eight-sided wood center hub on a table saw yourself, or have a woodworker make it for you. Use metal joist hangers (see page 99) or U-brackets to secure 2 by 4 spacers to the hub; then drill and bolt pairs of sloped 2 by 4 rafters to the spacers as shown at left. Also bolt rafters to the posts. Nail equally spaced 1 by 3 roof slats to the rafter tops. Finally, fasten the 1 by 3 wall louvers in place, leaving more or less space as your plants—and your desire for privacy—dictate.

Apple tree arbor

LIVING ARBORS

Wood and metal structures aren't your only arbor options. Why not let the plants do the work?

Pleaching trees—weaving their branches together to form a hedge or arbor—is a garden technique often associated with formal landscapes. But the same technique can create a rustic arbor like that shown above. To fashion this living structure, the owner planted eight 'Anna' apple trees 4½ feet apart in a circle about 12 feet across. Then she trained their branches to form a leafy roof, creating a living gazebo. (If she had to do it over again, she would expand the circle of trees to 14 feet across.) Plastic tape secures the top of each tree to a wire, which is in turn affixed to a center pole. The trees' straight trunks and long, flexible branches take to this treatment quite well. Chamomile forms a fragrant carpet beneath the circle of trees.

The arch of Italian cypresses shown at left spans walkway steps. The owners chose this living green arch over a wood or iron one, attracted both by its softer look and by its considerably lower cost. They started with trees from 5-gallon containers; these took about a year to grow tall enough to be tied together at the top with 12-gauge copper wire. The arch needs some pruning to maintain and improve its shape, but the job isn't an onerous one.

The sweet peas that twine their way up the green arch will be replaced by cypress vine (also known as cardinal climber) once they have run their course. Any lightweight vine would work here, though; you might choose hyacinth bean or climbing nasturtiums, for example. But vigorous vines like common morning glory are too heavy for a living arch to support.

Cypress arch

NUTS AND

BOLTS

Psst! Want to know a secret? There are plenty of people in the world who don't know what a 2 by 4 or a finish nail looks like, or how lumber is graded, or how to cut curves and drill straight holes. If you've wondered about these sorts of things, too, you're in luck—they're the subject of this chapter. The following pages present some tricks of the trade particular to trellis and arbor projects.

We begin with a look at lumber types and terms; show you options for fasteners and hardware; survey frequently used tools; demonstrate techniques for cutting and assembly; and finish up with finishes. Use the information here as a reference primer for the types of tasks required in Chapter 3, "Trellis Projects," and Chapter 4, "Arbor Ideas." If you're truly befuddled, you might want to consult the Sunset *titles* Basic Carpentry *or* Basic Woodworking *for help.*

A portable saber saw helps make some arbor-building tasks easier.
Here we're cutting the notches in one of the decorative beams shown on page 79.

LUMBER

Most arbor and trellis projects begin with lumber. And since wood takes the biggest bite out of your project budget, it pays to learn the basics of lumber types and terms before you shop. This section will introduce you to the characteristics of different kinds of lumber and explain how wood is sized, graded, and priced.

WHAT TYPE IS BEST?

For starters, lumber is divided into softwood and hardwood. These terms refer to the origin of the wood: softwoods come from conifers, hardwoods from deciduous trees. As a rule, softwoods are much less expensive and more readily available than hardwoods.

Woods from different trees have specific properties. For example, redwood and cedar heartwoods—the darker part of the wood, from the tree's core—are naturally resistant to decay. This characteristic (combined with their beauty) makes them ideal candidates for arbors and trellises—but because they're costly and limited in supply, many landscape professionals use less expensive woods, such as Douglas fir or western larch, for the structural or hidden parts of an outdoor structure. You can also apply a protective finish to make wood more durable (see page 106). Using pressure-treated lumber is another way to reduce cost; for details, see the facing page.

SURFACED, ROUGH, OR RESAWN?

Surfaced lumber, which has been planed smooth, is the standard for most construction and a must for decking. It is available in a range of grades (see facing page). Some lumberyards also carry rough lumber, but typically only in lower grades, with a correspondingly greater number of defects and higher moisture content. Resawn lumber has a texture that's rustic yet not too rough. Any grade can be resawn—a benefit where higher grades are needed for strength. And resawn lumber accepts stains beautifully.

LUMBER SIZES

Lumber is divided into categories according to size. Dimension lumber is nominally 2 to 4 inches thick and at least 2 inches wide; timbers are heavy structural lumber at least 5 inches thick; boards are usually not more than 1 inch thick and 4 to 12 inches wide.

Strictly speaking, outdoor lath is rough-surfaced redwood or cedar with dimensions of about ⅜ inch by 1½ inches; it's sold in lengths of 4, 6, and 8 feet, often in bundles of 50 pieces. In a broader sense, the word "lath" can refer to any rough or surfaced

TOP: Grades of redwood range from rough and knotty (left) to clear (far right). Higher grades are more attractive and (because they contain higher percentages of heartwood) more decay resistant.

slat up to about 1 by 2 size. Redwood and pine moldings fit the bill, too, but they can be pricey. Remember that a 2 by 4 does not actually measure 2 by 4 inches; "2 by 4" is its nominal size, designated before the wood is dried and surface-planed. The finished size is actually about 1½ by 3½ inches. Likewise, a 4 by 4 is actually about 3½ by 3½ inches.

Rough lumber is usually closer to the nominal size, since it's wetter and has not been surface-planed. When measurements are critical, be sure to check the actual dimensions of any lumber you are considering before you buy it.

Whether rough or surfaced, lumber is sold by either the lineal foot or the board foot. The lineal foot, commonly used for small orders, considers only length. For example, twenty 2 by 4s, 8 feet long, would be the same as 160 lineal feet of 2 by 4s.

The board foot is the most common unit for volume orders. A piece of wood 1 inch thick, 1 foot wide, and 1 foot long equals one board foot. To compute board feet, use this formula:

Nominal thickness (in inches) × nominal width (in feet) × length (in feet). So a 10-foot-long 1 by 6 is computed as follows:

1 inch × ½ foot (6 inches) × 10 feet = 5 board feet

When you place an order at a lumberyard, you still must give the exact dimensions of the lumber you need.

LUMBER GRADES

Structural lumber and timbers are rated for strength. The most common grading system includes the grades Select Structural, No. 1, No. 2, and No. 3. For premium strength, choose Select Structural. Often, lumberyards sell a mix of grades called No. 2 and Better. Other grading systems used for some lumber (typically 2 by 4s) classify wood according to the grades Construction, Standard, and Utility, or as a mixture of grades called Standard or Better.

Redwood is usually graded for its appearance and its percentage of heartwood. Clear All Heart is the best and the most expensive. B Heart, Construction Heart, and Merchantable Heart, in descending order of quality, are typical grades of pure heartwood; grades lower than these are likely to contain increasing numbers of knots, splits, and other flaws.

Cedar grades, starting with the highest quality, are Architect Clear, Custom Clear, Architect Knotty, and Custom Knotty. These grades don't indicate if the wood is heartwood.

The higher the grade, the more you will usually have to pay. One of the best ways to save money on a project is to identify and use the most appropriate—not the costliest—grade for each element; you'll find that you don't need to use the highest grade of lumber for the entire structure.

PRESSURE-TREATED LUMBER

Though redwood and cedar heartwoods are naturally resistant to decay and termites, most other woods soon rot and weaken if they come in prolonged contact with soil or water. To solve this problem, less durable types of lumber (such as southern pine and western hem-fir) are often factory-treated with chemical preservatives that guard against rot, insects, and other sources of decay. These woods are less expensive than redwood or cedar, and in some areas they're more readily available. They can be used for trellis frames (though small sizes are hard to find) and for structural arbor members such as posts, beams, and rafters.

Pressure-treated wood is available in two "exposures." For lumber that will be close to the ground, the Ground Contact type is required. Use the Above Ground type for other applications.

Working with treated lumber has its drawbacks. Unlike redwood and cedar, which are easy to cut and drive fasteners into, treated wood can be hard and brittle, and it can warp and twist. Moreover, some people object to the greenish color (though applying paint or a semitransparent stain can take care of this) and the staplelike incisions that usually cover its surface (some newer types come without these marks).

The primary preservative used in pressure-treated lumber contains chromium, a toxic metal. As a precaution, wear safety glasses and a dust mask when cutting this type of lumber, and wear gloves when handling it for prolonged periods. And never burn the scraps.

FASTENERS AND HARDWARE

Nails, screws, and framing connectors are essential for outdoor projects: without them, it would be difficult to put boards or beams together!

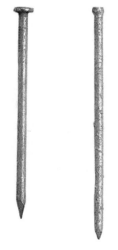

Common   Finish
nail   nail

NAILS

Hot-dipped galvanized, aluminum, or stainless steel nails are best for outdoor construction, because they assure rust resistance. As far as type of nail goes, you can use common or finish nails. Heavy-duty common nails have a head and a thick shank—a feature that makes them more difficult to drive but increases their holding power.

Choose a finish nail when the head shouldn't show; drive it nearly flush, then sink the rounded head with a nailset. Both common and finish nails are sold in 1-, 5-, and 50-pound boxes, or loose in bins. Standard nail sizes are given in "pennies," with the word "penny" abbreviated as "d" (from the Latin *denarius*, a type of Roman coin). The higher the penny number, the longer the nail. Equivalents in inches for the most frequently used nails are as follows:

3d = 1¼ inches   8d = 2½ inches

4d = 1½ inches   10d = 3 inches

6d = 2 inches   16d = 3½ inches

Choose nails about twice as long as the thickness of the material you'll be nailing through. Most arbor framing is secured with 8d and 16d nails.

SCREWS

Though they're more expensive than nails, coated or galvanized screws offer several advantages. They don't pop out as readily as nails, and their coating is less likely to be damaged during installation; and since they aren't pounded in, you don't have to worry about hammer dents. They're also easier to remove than nails when repairs are required.

Galvanized deck screws are surprisingly easy to drive into softwoods (such as redwood or cedar) if you use an electric drill or screw gun with an adjustable clutch and a Phillips screwdriver tip. Drywall screws (so-called multipurpose screws), usually black in color, come in smaller sizes than deck screws but are less weather resistant. These two types of screws are not given ratings for shear (or hanging) strength, so it's best to use nails, lag screws, or bolts to fasten rafters to beams or ledgers and to join posts to beams.

Choose screws that are long enough to penetrate about twice the top member's thickness (for example, use 2½-inch screws to join two 2 by 4s or 2 by 6s). Screws are sold loose (by the pound) or in boxes ranging from small to 25-pound size; the bigger boxes offer a substantial savings.

The heavy-duty lag screw (lag bolt) has a square or hexagonal head and must be tightened with a wrench or a ratchet and socket.

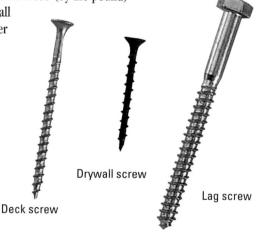

Deck screw   Drywall screw   Lag screw

Machine bolt

Carriage bolt

Expanding anchors

BOLTS

For heavy-duty fastening, choose bolts. Most are zinc-plated steel, but aluminum and brass ones are also available. Bolts go into predrilled holes and are secured by nuts. The machine bolt has a square or hexagonal head, a nut, and two washers; it must be tightened with a wrench at each end. The carriage bolt has a self-anchoring head that digs into the wood as the nut is tightened. Expanding anchors allow you to secure wooden members to a masonry wall.

Bolts are classified by diameter (⅛ to 1 inch) and length (⅜ inch and up). To give the nut a firm bite, select a bolt ½ to 1 inch longer than the combined thicknesses of the pieces to be joined.

FRAMING CONNECTORS

The photos below show several framing connectors. Galvanized metal connectors can help prevent lumber splits caused by "toe-nailing" (see page 104) two boards together. Connectors handy for arbor building include post anchors, post caps, joist hangers, rafter ties, and a variety of reinforcing straps. Be sure to attach connectors with the nails specified by the manufacturer; they are shorter and fatter than standard nails.

ADHESIVES

To prevent trellis rungs or arbor elements from working loose, you can use adhesive in addition to nails or screws. Keep in mind, however, that glued-together pieces will be very difficult to remove if you should later need to disassemble part of the structure for repairs.

Some adhesives are designed specifically for outdoor construction such as decking or siding; these usually come in long cartridges and are applied with a caulking gun. Alternatively, you can use a waterproof adhesive such as resorcinol, epoxy, polyurethane, or exterior-rated "yellow" (aliphatic resin) glue.

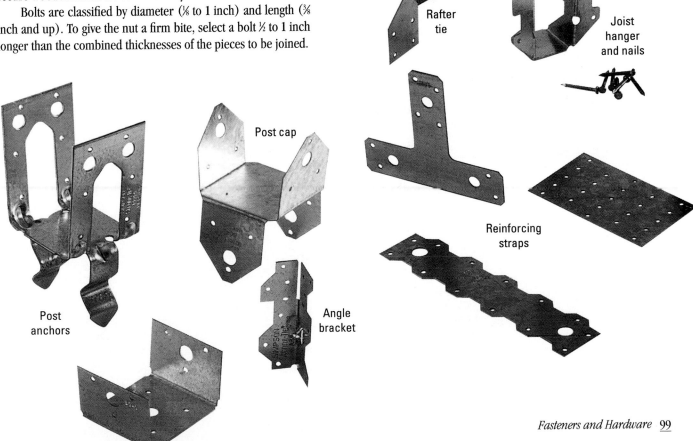

Rafter tie

Joist hanger and nails

Post cap

Post anchors

Angle bracket

Reinforcing straps

A GARDEN BUILDER'S TOOLKIT

Most arbor and trellis projects can be built with just a few modest tools. In fact, the contents of an average home repair kit may be all you need. However, some specialized hand and power tools will let you do the job more quickly, easily, and accurately, especially if the structure is a large one.

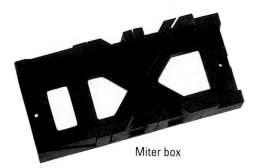

Coping saw

Miter box

![Backsaw image]

Backsaw

HAND TOOLS

A collection of basic tools is outlined below. You may already have most or all of these, but if you're shopping, this information can point you in the right direction.

Steel measuring tape. A simple 6-foot tape may be all you need for a small trellis, but for larger jobs, consider a ¾- or 1-inch-wide tape that's 16 or 25 feet long. Wider tapes won't twist and buckle, so you can extend them over longer distances.

Square. A square helps you draw straight lines across lumber to be cut; it also helps check angles on assembled pieces of the structure. A basic, fixed try square will do, but an adjustable combination square is more useful. An adjustable T-bevel helps lay out angles.

Hammer. Choose a 12- to 16-ounce curved-claw hammer for general work and a 20-ounce straight-claw model for framing (it packs a bigger wallop for longer nails). The face should be smooth, not serrated, to minimize any dings you might make in the wood (or in your thumb!).

Plumb bob or mason's line. You probably won't need to string lines for a simple trellis, but some overheads require a reference point when you're lining up posts or transferring layout lines from ground to overhead beams.

Level. A carpenter's level, typically 2 feet long, helps check an arbor or trellis for both level and plumb; a 4-foot mason's level is even handier. To check level across longer distances, consider a line level or water level (essentially a water-filled tube); new electronic versions emit a beep when the levels at both ends line up.

Chisel, block plane. Though not really essential, these basic carpenter's tools can be handy for cleaning up errant saw cuts and joints. The plastic-handled, metal-capped butt chisel can be driven by a hammer.

Crosscut saw. Unlike the specialized rip saw (used for "ripping" wood with the grain), a crosscut saw is designed to cut boards across their widths; it's also handy for cutting plywood. A good choice is a 26-inch blade with 8 points per inch. For finer work, you might want a backsaw, which is stiffer than a crosscut saw and has finer teeth (it's usually used with a miter box; see below).

Coping saw. Cutting curves is the coping saw's business. The wider the saw's throat, the farther in from a board's edge you can cut.

Miter box. Made from wood, metal, or plastic, this troughlike frame has various standard angles cut in its sides to guide your saw blade. You can use most versions with a standard crosscut saw or a backsaw.

Pliers. A pair of 9- or 10-inch lineman's pliers with wire cutters will twist and cut wire and pull out errant fasteners. Locking pliers are another option.

Wrench. An adjustable wrench is good for many bolt or nut sizes, but not as precise as a box or open-end wrench. A ratchet-and-socket set may be required to reach into a countersunk bolt hole (see page 104) while tightening.

Clamps. When you feel like you need an extra pair of hands, what you really need is a clamp. Clamps hold things where you want them; they're also essential for holding some parts together while glue dries. C-clamps are the old standby; bar clamps have a longer reach. The spring clamp, which looks like an oversize clothespin, is inexpensive and great for small jobs.

POWER TOOLS

The following portable power tools make large trellis or arbor projects go a lot faster, and in the hands of the average do-it-yourselfer, they produce better results than hand tools. There are also big, expensive stationary power tools to be had—and if you have access to a table saw, radial-arm saw, or band saw, you'll find they're great for some stages of arbor building that can be completed in the shop or garage.

Electric drill and bits

Electric drill and bits. This power tool has all but replaced hand drills and screw-drivers (at least when more than a couple of screws are involved). Look for a ⅜-inch reversible drill; cordless models are very handy. To bore holes up to ½ inch in diameter, use standard twist bits; for larger holes, use spade bits. A carbide-tipped masonry bit can tackle stucco siding. When fitted with a Phillips-head tip, the drill is equally handy as a power screwdriver, but you'll need a variable-speed model or screws will strip. Models with an adjustable clutch prevent screws from being driven too deep.

Portable circular saw. This does the same job as a handsaw, but much more quickly. Equipped with a combination blade, it can handle both crosscuts and rip cuts (with the grain). The 7¼-inch size is standard.

Portable circular saw

Saber saw/jigsaw. This is the electric version of the hand-powered coping saw; it can be used for both straight and delicately curved cuts. Unlike a coping saw, the saber saw can make cuts well away from an edge, and it even makes interior "pocket" cuts if you drill an access hole first. Choose the right blade for the job: thin, fine-tooth blades for tight curves, beefier ones for rougher, straighter cuts.

Router. The electric router makes short work of grooves, rabbets (grooves along an edge), and the decorative edge treatments that can spice up a basic project—chamfers (bevels) and roundovers (rounded edges), for example. Look for a router rated for at least one horsepower. Popular router bits include straight, rabbeting, chamfering, and roundover bits.

Miter saw. Also called a chop saw, the miter saw is the power version of the good old backsaw and miter box. It excels at making clean, accurate angle cuts; if your project requires a lot of angles or detail work, you might consider renting one. A 10-inch miter saw is standard. So-called compound miter saws cut angles in two directions at once, a feature that's sometimes handy for rafters or fancy trim. Sliding miter saws can cut stock up to about a foot wide.

Saber saw

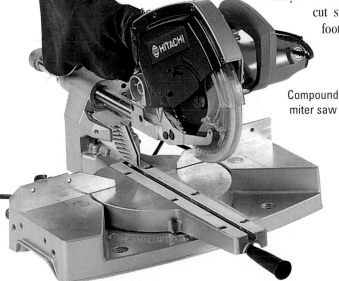

Compound miter saw

Router

TRICKS OF THE TRADE

The typical arbor or trellis project requires only basic carpentry skills. Below, we review a few special techniques that can make the going easier. If you're completely unfamiliar with tasks such as measuring and cutting lumber and hammering nails, you might want to take a look at Sunset's Basic Carpentry.

SAW-CUT SAVVY

Whether you're using hand tools or portable power ones, it's sometimes hard to get a really straight cut. One solution is to clamp on a guide; any straight board or plywood piece will do. Use the straightedge to guide your handsaw or portable circular saw. In the case of the power saw, you'll first need to figure the distance from the edge of the saw's baseplate to its blade, then space the straightedge this distance from the line you are cutting.

Cutting all the way through a 4 by 4 post can be awkward. If you're using a handsaw, first mark the cutting line across the board, then use your square to extend it down both sides. Use these side lines to keep your saw on track. With a circular saw, you can only cut about half the depth at once. Either finish the cut with a handsaw (using the existing cut as a guide) or flip the 4 by 4 over and make another cut from the bottom, carefully matching saw kerfs. The handsaw is the easier option.

When it comes to angles, first mark the line to be cut with a combination square (45° angles only) or an adjustable T-bevel. If it's a standard angle like 30° or 45°, you can cut it using a miter box and handsaw; otherwise, you'll need to cut freehand. On a circular saw, either cut freehand (which can be tricky) or clamp on a guide, remembering to allow for the distance from baseplate to blade. Odd angles are a piece of cake for the power miter saw.

Curves are another matter. Cut them freehand with either a coping saw or a power saber saw. If the curve is uniform, lay it out using a compass or a French curve, or by first plotting it on paper, then enlarging it in a photocopier and cutting it out to make a template. If you are making more than one matching piece—say, decorative rafter tails or knee braces—cut the first one to your satisfaction, then use it to lay out the rest. Some saber saws include circle-cutting guides; the saw tracks around a central point. When cutting concentric circles (like a doughnut shape), make the inside cut first so you'll have plenty of stock left to support the saw during the outside cut.

CLOCKWISE FROM TOP RIGHT: A straightedge helps guide a portable circular saw; a miter box provides a 45° angle; a saber saw cuts speedy, accurate curves.

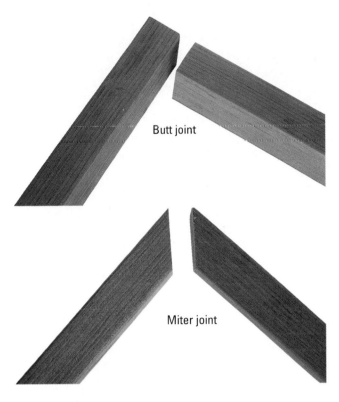

Butt joint

Miter joint

Lap joint

JOINERY 101

Most arbor and trellis projects call for simple butt joints; trim pieces are sometimes mitered. Both joints are shown above.

Butt joints have standard 90° ends. If one piece overlaps the other, driving nails or screws is easy. If the pieces join in a T, however, and you can't drive fasteners from behind, they can be awkward to join. Traditional "toenailing" can be exasperating,

since the part being secured tends to move off-line as you hammer. Screws are a bit easier to work with, especially if you drive angled pilot holes first. Clamps and blocks can hold pieces in line. However, framing connectors or L-brackets are easier to use at these junctions, and they also make a stronger joint; if you don't like the way they look, paint them.

Miter joints are cut at 45° angles. Make the cuts as described under "Saw-cut Savvy," on the facing page. End miters (like those you see at the corners of picture frames) are pretty straightforward. Edge miters are difficult to cut by hand unless the stock is narrow enough to fit upright in a miter box; for these, a sliding or compound miter saw, radial-arm saw, or table saw may be in order. You can also use a circular saw's bevel (side-tilt) adjustment, but cuts made this way are often imprecise.

Lap joints call for other techniques. A half-lap has a notch or groove cut in one piece; the corresponding piece sits inside this notch. A full-lap joint, where both pieces are of equal thickness, joins corresponding notches, each one-half the total depth. Again,

PLAY IT SAFE

Before you begin work, make sure you have the necessary safety equipment on hand. Wear goggles, safety glasses, or a face mask when operating power tools or using any striking tool. Wear a respirator to prevent breathing harmful vapors (such as those from oil-base finishes). A disposable painter's dust mask can protect you from heavy sawdust; it's essential when cutting pressure-treated lumber. Also wear earmuff hearing protectors or earplugs when operating power tools for any length of time. A hard hat offers protection when you're working beneath an overhead or working with others in close quarters.

Wear all-leather or leather-reinforced cotton work gloves to handle wood; wear rubber gloves when applying finishes and other caustic products. Sturdy work boots, especially the steel-toed sort, protect your feet from dropped blades, tools, or lumber.

When using a new tool, always read the owner's manual carefully and follow all safety directions. To guard against shock, power tools must be either double-insulated or grounded. Double-insulated tools, which contain a built-in second barrier of protective insulation, offer the best protection; they are clearly marked and should not be grounded (they have two-prong plugs only).

Since most of your work may take place outdoors, take special precautions against shock. A ground-fault circuit interrupter (GFCI), either portable or built into the outlet, is essential; it will cut the power within $\frac{1}{40}$ of a second after a leak in current.

To shape a lap joint's notch, first make repeated saw cuts, then clean out the "waste" with a sharp chisel.

it's a lot of work to cut these with a handsaw. If you use a portable circular saw, set the blade depth at one-half the piece's depth; make two cuts to outline the joint's shoulder, then several more cuts in the "waste area" inside the lines, as shown at left. Use a chisel to remove the waste and to smooth the joint's bottom. Sound tedious? It is! Using a radial-arm saw and a dado blade makes the process speedier and more straightforward.

FASTENING FACTS

Sometimes you really need to drill a clean, straight hole, especially when it will be highly visible. Two problems crop up: first, the hole may not be perpendicular; and second, the back of the hole (where the drill bit exits the wood) tears and splinters.

You can usually get a fairly straight hole simply by eyeballing the drill bit's angle as you go; if you like, place a square next to the drill to help you judge. If the hole really needs to be straight and you don't have a drill press (another pricey power tool) on hand, consider a portable drill guide that keeps the drill perpendicular.

There are also two solutions for ragged exit holes. You can temporarily attach a wood scrap behind the joint and drill clear into it (the block stops the tearout); or you can drill through just until the bit's tip starts to protrude, then flip the piece and finish drilling from the back.

Deck and drywall screws have sharp points and aggressive threads, so you shouldn't need to drill pilot holes to drive them into redwood or other softwoods. But if they aren't cooperating or if you're splitting the wood when fastening near an end, choose a drill bit slightly smaller than the screw and drill a pilot hole to about three-fourths the screw's length.

Lag screws and machine bolts often look better if countersunk (with their heads below the wood's surface). Use a spade bit to make the countersink; size it just slightly larger than the fastener's washer and drill just deeper than the fastener's head. Then drill a second, smaller pilot hole for the fastener itself through the center of the countersink hole. For lag screws, make this second pilot hole

To countersink a machine bolt, first drill a large, shallow hole for the fastener's head and washer; then drill a smaller shank hole clear through the wood.

the same diameter as the shank between the screw threads (the threads need to "bite" into the wood) and drill it to about two-thirds the length of the screw. Start the lag screw with a few hammer blows, then drive it tight with a wrench or ratchet. If it won't go in, make the pilot hole longer. For bolts, drill a hole just slightly larger than the shank (the bolt must slide freely inside it) and all the way through the joint.

Use two wrenches to secure a machine bolt: one on the head, another on the nut to keep it from twirling. Carriage bolts require just one wrench, on the nut; the head should stay put.

GETTING FANCY

The decorative details suggested for some of our projects are best done with an electric router and the appropriate bit. Most edge details—like chamfers, rabbets, and roundovers—are fashioned with corresponding bits; these all come with pilot bushings that guide the bit along an edge. Do this sort of detailing before assembling the pieces. You can also cut rabbets using a table saw and dado blade, but long pieces are more easily handled with the router.

Decorative edge details are the router's specialty. Shown here, from top to bottom, are a chamfer, a rabbet, and a roundover.

STRONG TIES

A trellis needs solid support to do its job. You can anchor one to a wall, a fence, to overhanging house eaves, or the side of an arbor. Freestanding trellises may be secured to the ground via sturdy stakes; or, in the case of those with posts, directly to a buried concrete footing.

Generally, it's easy to attach a trellis to a wooden fence or to wood house siding. Use rust-resistant nails, screws, or—for heavy structures—lag screws. Spacer blocks keep trellis away from wood, providing breathing room for both plants and wood. If your trellis is beefy, you'll want to drive these fasteners into wall framing or posts, not just thin siding or fence boards.

Masonry walls can be trickier. The surest method is to insert expanding anchors (shown on page 99) into holes drilled in the wall's stucco, brick, or block surface; a galvanized screw or lag screw threads into the anchor. Concrete screws can secure light trellises.

A tall, house-attached trellis can stretch from near ground level to the roof overhang: plan to bolt or screw the top of these structures to rafter extensions. You'll need to design the trellis width to meet at least two rafter tails, or to meet a top piece fastened between them.

Freestanding, lightweight grids will last longer if they do not contact the ground directly. Instead, consider driving a pressure-treated wood stake, a length of steel reinforcing bar, or a galvanized pipe sleeve into the ground. Then fasten the trellis to the stake, using screws, bolts, or wire.

Heavier trellises with integral posts should be buried in a hole at least 1½ feet deep (or below the local frost line). For portability, you can fill this hole with packed gravel or sand; but for maximum strength, plan on setting posts in concrete or fastening them to a post anchor that's in turn held by concrete. For additional details, see page 107.

FINISHING TOUCHES

Structural elements that contact soil or are embedded in concrete do not require a finish. But to protect the rest of a structure and preserve its beauty, you'll want to apply a water repellent, a semi-transparent or solid-color stain, or paint. Whatever product you choose, try it on a sample board first. And always read labels: some products should not be applied over new wood, and others may require a sealer first.

Water repellents (water sealers) help keep wood from warping and cracking. They may be clear or slightly tinted; the clear sorts do not color the wood, instead letting it fade gradually to gray. You can buy either oil- or water-base products, many of which include UV-blockers and mildewcides.

Don't use clear-surface finishes such as spar varnish or polyurethane on outdoor lumber. Besides being expensive, they wear quickly and are very hard to renew.

Available in both water- and oil-base versions, semitransparent stains contain enough pigment to tint the wood's surface with just one coat, while still letting the natural grain show through. You'll find traditional grays and wood tones as well as products to "revive" an unpainted structure's natural wood color or dress up pressure-treated wood.

To cover a structure in a solid color, you can choose either stain or paint. Stains for siding or decking are essentially thin paints; they cover the wood grain completely. For custom tints, you can usually mix any paint color you choose into this base.

Paints cover wood in an opaque coat of muted to vibrant color. Because they hide defects so thoroughly, they let you use lower grades of lumber. Most painters recommend a two-step procedure for outdoor structures: you first apply an alkyd- or oil-base prime coat, then follow it with one or two topcoats of water-base (latex) enamel. Ideally, the primer should cover all surfaces of the lumber (including the inner faces of built-up posts, beams, or rafters), so it's best to prime before assembly. Apply topcoats after the structure is complete.

Heavy-bodied stains may be either brushed or sprayed on; paint can be applied with a brush, roller, or spray gun. When it comes to complex shapes like lath and lattice, spraying is the easiest way to do the job.

Shown above, from top to bottom: unfinished redwood; clear water sealer; tinted oil-base repellent; gray semitransparent stain; and red solid-color stain.

SOME CONCRETE FACTS

Typically, posts for arbors and overheads rest on piers embedded in poured concrete footings. Although many people think concrete is just "cement," it is actually a combination of portland cement, sand, aggregate (usually gravel), and water. Portland cement is a complex, finely ground material that undergoes a chemical reaction when mixed with water, becoming a sort of glue that binds all the other elements together. It also gives the finished product its hardness. The sand and aggregate act as fillers and control shrinkage.

Bagged dry, ready-mixed concrete is expensive but convenient, especially for small jobs. The standard 90-pound bag makes ⅔ cubic foot of concrete, enough to fill one post hole or to cover a 16-inch-square area 4 inches deep.

If your project is fairly large, order materials in bulk and mix them yourself, either by hand or with a power mixer. Use 1 part cement, 2 parts clean river sand, and 3 parts gravel. Add clean water, a little at a time, as you mix. The concrete should be plastic but not runny.

You can dig postholes with a pick and shovel, but using heavier equipment will save time and effort. A posthole (clamshell) digger (shown near right) works in hard or rocky soil. Spread the handles to open and close the blades, which trap soil. Posthole diggers are difficult to use for holes deeper than 3 feet, because the hole's sides make it hard to spread the tool's handles.

When you turn the handle of a hand-operated auger, the pointed blades bore into the soil, scraping it up and collecting it in a chamber. Once the chamber is full, remove the auger from the hole and empty out the soil. This tool works best in loose soil.

A power auger, also known as a power digger or earth drill, is recommended whenever you have more than a dozen holes to dig. You can rent models for operation by one or two people (a two-person model is shown at far right); they may be freestanding or vehicle-mounted. Every so often, pull the auger out of the hole to remove the dirt; a posthole digger or a small spade may also be required.

Power auger

Posthole digger

SUNSET'S GARDEN CLIMATE ZONES

A plant's performance is governed by the total climate: length of growing season, timing and amount of rainfall, winter lows, summer highs, humidity. *Sunset's* climate zone maps take all these factors into account—unlike the familiar hardiness zone maps devised by the U.S. Department of Agriculture, which divide the U.S. and Canada into zones based strictly on winter lows. The U.S.D.A. maps tell you only where a plant may survive the winter; our climate zone maps let you see where that plant will thrive year-round. Below are brief descriptions of the 45 zones illustrated on the map on pages 110–111. For more information, consult *Sunset's National Garden Book* and *Western Garden Book*.

ZONE 1. Coldest Winters in the West and Western Prairie States

Growing season: early June through Aug., but with some variation—the longest seasons are usually found near this zone's large bodies of water. Frost can come any night of the year. Winters are snowy and intensely cold, due to latitude, elevation, and/or influence of continental air mass. There's some summer rainfall.

ZONE 2. Second-coldest Western Climate

Growing season: early May through Sept. Winters are cold (lows run from −3° to −34°F/−19° to −37°C), but less so than in Zone 1. In northern and interior areas, lower elevations fall into Zone 2, higher areas into Zone 1.

ZONE 3. West's Mildest High-elevation and Interior Regions

Growing season: early May to late Sept.—shorter than in Zone 2, but offset by milder winters (lows from 13° to −24°F/−11° to −31°C). This is fine territory for plants needing winter chill and dry, hot summers.

ZONE 4. Cold-winter Western Washington and British Columbia

Growing season: early May to early Oct. Summers are cool, thanks to ocean influence; chilly winters (19° to −7°F/−7° to −22°C) result from elevation, influence of continental air mass, or both. Coolness, ample rain suit many perennials and bulbs.

ZONE 5. Ocean-influenced Northwest Coast and Puget Sound

Growing season: mid-April to Nov., typically with cool temperatures throughout. Less rain falls here than in Zone 4; winter lows range from 28° to 1°F/−2° to −17°C. This "English garden" climate is ideal for rhododendrons and many rock garden plants.

ZONE 6. Oregon's Willamette Valley

Growing season: mid-Mar. to mid-Nov., with somewhat warmer temperatures than in Zone 5. Ocean influence keeps winter lows about the same as in Zone 5. Climate suits all but tender plants and those needing hot or dry summers.

ZONE 7. Oregon's Rogue River Valley, California's High Foothills

Growing season: May to early Oct. Summers are hot and dry; typical winter lows run from 23° to 9°F/−5° to −13°C. The summer-winter contrast suits plants that need dry, hot summers and moist, only moderately cold winters.

ZONE 8. Cold-air Basins of California's Central Valley

Growing season: mid-Feb. through Nov. This is a valley floor with no maritime influence. Summers are hot; winter lows range from 29° to 13°F/−2° to −11°C. Rain comes in the cooler months, covering just the early part of the growing season.

ZONE 9. Thermal Belts of California's Central Valley

Growing season: late Feb. through Dec. Zone 9 is located in the higher elevations around Zone 8, but its summers are just as hot; its winter lows are slightly higher (temperatures range from 28° to 18°F/−2° to −8°C). Rainfall pattern is the same as in Zone 8.

ZONE 10. High Desert Areas of Arizona, New Mexico, West Texas, Oklahoma Panhandle, and Southwest Kansas

Growing season: April to early Nov. Chilly (even snow-dusted) weather rules from late Nov. through Feb., with lows from 31° to 24°F/−1° to −4°C. Rain comes in summer as well as in the cooler seasons.

ZONE 11. Medium to High Desert of California and Southern Nevada

Growing season: early April to late Oct. Summers are sizzling, with 110 days above 90°F/32°C. Balancing this is a 3½-month winter, with 85 nights below freezing and lows from 11° to 0°F/−12° to −18°C. Scant rainfall comes in winter.

ZONE 12. Arizona's Intermediate Desert

Growing season: mid-Mar. to late Nov., with scorching midsummer heat. Compared to Zone 13, this region has harder frosts; record low is 6°F/−14°C. Rains come in summer and winter.

ZONE 13. Low or Subtropical Desert

Growing season: mid-Feb. through Nov., interrupted by nearly 3 months of incandescent, growth-stopping summer heat. Most frosts are light (record lows run from 19° to 13°F/−17° to −11°C); scant rain comes in summer and winter.

ZONE 14. Inland Northern and Central California with Some Ocean Influence

Growing season: early Mar. to mid-Nov., with rain coming in the remaining months. Periodic intrusions of marine air temper summer heat and winter cold (lows run from 26° to 16°F/−3° to −9°C). Mediterranean-climate plants are at home here.

ZONE 15. Northern and Central California's Chilly-winter Coast-influenced Areas

Growing season: Mar. to Dec. Rain comes from fall through winter. Typical winter lows range from 28° to 21°F/−2° to −6°C. Maritime air influences the zone much of the time, giving it cooler, moister summers than Zone 14.

ZONE 16. Northern and Central California Coast Range Thermal Belts

Growing season: late Feb. to late Nov. With cold air draining to lower elevations, winter lows typically run from 32° to 19°F/0° to −7°C. Like Zone 15, this region is dominated by maritime air, but its winters are milder on average.

ZONE 17. Oceanside Northern and Central California and Southernmost Oregon

Growing season: late Feb. to early Dec. Coolness and fog are hallmarks; summer highs seldom top 75°F/24°C, while winter lows run from 36° to 23°F/2° to −5°C. Heat-loving plants disappoint or dwindle here.

ZONE 18. Hilltops and Valley Floors of Interior Southern California

Growing season: mid-Mar. through late Nov. Summers are hot and dry; rain comes in winter, when lows reach 28° to 10°F/−2° to −12°C. Plants from the Mediterranean and Near Eastern regions thrive here.

ZONE 19. Thermal belts around Southern California's Interior Valleys

Growing season: early Mar. through Nov. As in Zone 18, rainy winters and hot, dry summers are the norm—but here, winter lows dip only to 27° to 22°F/−3° to −6°C, allowing some tender evergreen plants to grow outdoors with protection.

ZONE 20. Hilltops and Valley Floors of Ocean-influenced Inland Southern California

Growing season: late Mar. to late Nov.—but fairly mild winters (lows of 28° to 23°F/−2° to −5°C) allow gardening through much of the year. Cool and moist maritime influence alternates with hot, dry interior air.

ZONE 21. Thermal Belts around Southern California's Ocean-influenced Interior Valleys

Growing season: early Mar. to early Dec., with the same tradeoff of oceanic and interior influence as in Zone 20. During the winter rainy season, lows range from 36° to 23°F/2° to −5°C—warmer than in Zone 20, since the colder air drains to the valleys.

ZONE 22. Colder-winter Parts of Southern California's Coastal Region

Growing season: Mar. to early Dec. Winter lows seldom fall below 28°F/–2°C (records are around 21°F/–6°C), though colder air sinks to this zone from Zone 23. Summers are warm; rain comes in winter. Climate here is largely oceanic.

ZONE 23. Thermal Belts of Southern California's Coastal Region

Growing season: almost year-round (all but first half of Jan.). Rain comes in winter. Reliable ocean influence keeps summers mild (except when hot Santa Ana winds come from inland), frosts negligible; 23°F/–5°C is the record low.

ZONE 24. Marine-dominated Southern California Coast

Growing season: all year, but periodic freezes have dramatic effects (record lows are 33° to 20°F/1° to –7°C). Climate here is oceanic (but warmer than oceanic Zone 17), with cool summers, mild winters. Subtropical plants thrive.

ZONE 25. South Florida and the Keys

Growing season: all year. Add ample year-round rainfall (least in Dec. through Mar.), high humidity, and overall warmth, and you have a near-tropical climate. The Keys are frost-free; winter lows elsewhere run from 40° to 25°F/4° to –4°C.

ZONE 26. Central and Interior Florida

Growing season: early Feb. to late Dec., with typically humid, warm to hot weather. Rain is plentiful all year, heaviest in summer and early fall. Lows range from 15°F/–9°C in the north to 27°F/–3°C in the south; arctic air brings periodic hard freezes.

ZONE 27. Lower Rio Grande Valley

Growing season: early Mar. to mid-Dec.. Summers are hot and humid; winter lows only rarely dip below freezing. Many plants from tropical and subtropical Africa and South America are well adapted here.

ZONE 28. Gulf Coast, North Florida, Atlantic Coast to Charleston

Growing season: mid-Mar. to early Dec. Humidity and rainfall are year-round phenomena; summers are hot, winters virtually frostless but subject to periodic invasions by frigid arctic air. Azaleas, camellias, many subtropicals flourish.

ZONE 29. Interior Plains of South Texas

Growing season: mid-Mar. through Nov. Moderate rainfall (to 25" annually) comes year-round. Summers are hot. Winter lows can dip to 26°F/–3°C, with occasional arctic freezes bringing much lower readings.

ZONE 30. Hill Country of Central Texas

Growing season: mid-Mar. through Nov. Zone 30 has higher annual rainfall than Zone 29 (to 35") and lower winter temperatures, normally to around 20°F/–7°C. Seasonal variations favor many fruit crops, perennials.

ZONE 31. Interior Plains of Gulf Coast and Coastal Southeast

Growing season: mid-Mar. to early Nov. In this extensive east-west zone, hot and sticky summers contrast with chilly winters (record low temperatures are 7° to 0°F/–14° to –18°C). There's rain all year (an annual average of 50"), with the least falling in Oct.

ZONE 32. Interior Plains of Mid-Atlantic States; Chesapeake Bay, Southeastern Pennsylvania, Southern New Jersey

Growing season: late Mar. to early Nov. Rain falls year-round (40" to 50" annually); winter lows (moving through the zone from south to north) are 30° to 20°F/–1° to –7°C. Humidity is less oppressive here than in Zone 31.

ZONE 33. North-Central Texas and Oklahoma Eastward to the Appalachian Foothills

Growing season: mid-April through Oct. Warm Gulf Coast air and colder continental/arctic fronts both play a role; their unpredictable interplay results in a wide range in annual rainfall (22" to 52") and winter lows (20° to 0°F/–7° to –18°C). Summers are muggy and warm to hot.

ZONE 34. Lowlands and Coast from Gettysburg to North of Boston

Growing season: late April to late Oct. Ample rainfall and humid summers are the norm. Winters are variable—typically fairly mild (around 20°F/–7°C), but with lows down to –3° to –22°F/–19° to –30°C if arctic air swoops in.

ZONE 35. Ouachita Mountains, Northern Oklahoma and Arkansas, Southern Kansas to North-Central Kentucky and Southern Ohio

Growing season: late April to late Oct. Rain comes in all seasons. Summers can be truly hot and humid. Without arctic fronts, winter lows are around 10°F/–8°C, with them, the coldest weather may bring lows of –20°F/–29°C.

ZONE 36. Appalachian Mountains

Growing season: May to late Oct. Thanks to greater elevation, summers are cooler and less humid, winters colder (0° to –20°F/–18° to –29°C) than in adjacent, lower zones. Rain comes all year (heaviest in spring). Late frosts are common.

ZONE 37. Hudson Valley and Appalachian Plateau

Growing season: May to mid-Oct., with rainfall throughout. Lower in elevation than neighboring Zone 42, with warmer winters: lows are 0° to –5°F/–18° to –21°C, unless arctic air moves in. Summer is warm to hot, humid.

ZONE 38. New England Interior and Lowland Maine

Growing season: May to early Oct. Summers feature reliable rainfall and lack oppressive humidity of lower-elevation, more southerly areas. Winter lows dip to –10° to –20°F/–23° to –29°C, with periodic colder temperatures due to influxes of arctic air.

ZONE 39. Shoreline Regions of the Great Lakes

Growing season: early May to early Oct. Springs and summers are cooler here, autumns milder than in areas farther from the lakes. Southeast lakeshores get the heaviest snowfalls. Lows reach 0° to –10°F/–18° to –23°C.

ZONE 40. Inland Plains of Lake Erie and Lake Ontario

Growing season: mid-May to mid-Sept., with rainy, warm, variably humid weather. The lakes help moderate winter lows; temperatures typically range from –10° to –20°F/–23° to –29°C, with occasional colder readings when arctic fronts rush through.

ZONE 41. Northeast Kansas and Southeast Nebraska to Northern Illinois and Indiana, Southeast Wisconsin, Michigan, Northern Ohio

Growing season: early May to early Oct. Winter brings average lows of –11° to –20°F/–23° to –29°C. Summers in this zone are hotter and longer west of the Mississippi, cooler and shorter nearer the Great Lakes; summer rainfall increases in the same west-to-east direction.

ZONE 42. Interior Pennsylvania and New York; St. Lawrence Valley

Growing season: late May to late Sept. This zone's elevation gives it colder winters than surrounding zones: lows range from –20° to –40°F/–29° to –40°C, with the colder readings coming in the Canadian portion of the zone. Summers are humid, rainy.

ZONE 43. Upper Mississippi Valley, Upper Michigan, Southern Ontario and Quebec

Growing season: late May to mid-Sept. The climate is humid from spring through early fall; summer rains are usually dependable. Arctic air dominates in winter, with lows typically from –20° to –30°F/–29° to –34°C.

ZONE 44. Mountains of New England and Southeastern Quebec

Growing season: June to mid-Sept. Latitude and elevation give fairly cool, rainy summers, cold winters with lows of –20° to –40°F/–29° to –40°C. Choose short-season, low heat-requirement annuals and vegetables.

ZONE 45. Northern Parts of Minnesota and Wisconsin, Eastern Manitoba through Interior Quebec

Growing season: mid-June through Aug., with rain throughout; rainfall (and humidity) are least in zone's western part, greatest in eastern reaches. Winters are frigid (–30° to –40°F/–34° to –40°C), with snow cover, deeply frozen soil.

Sunset's Garden Climate Zones

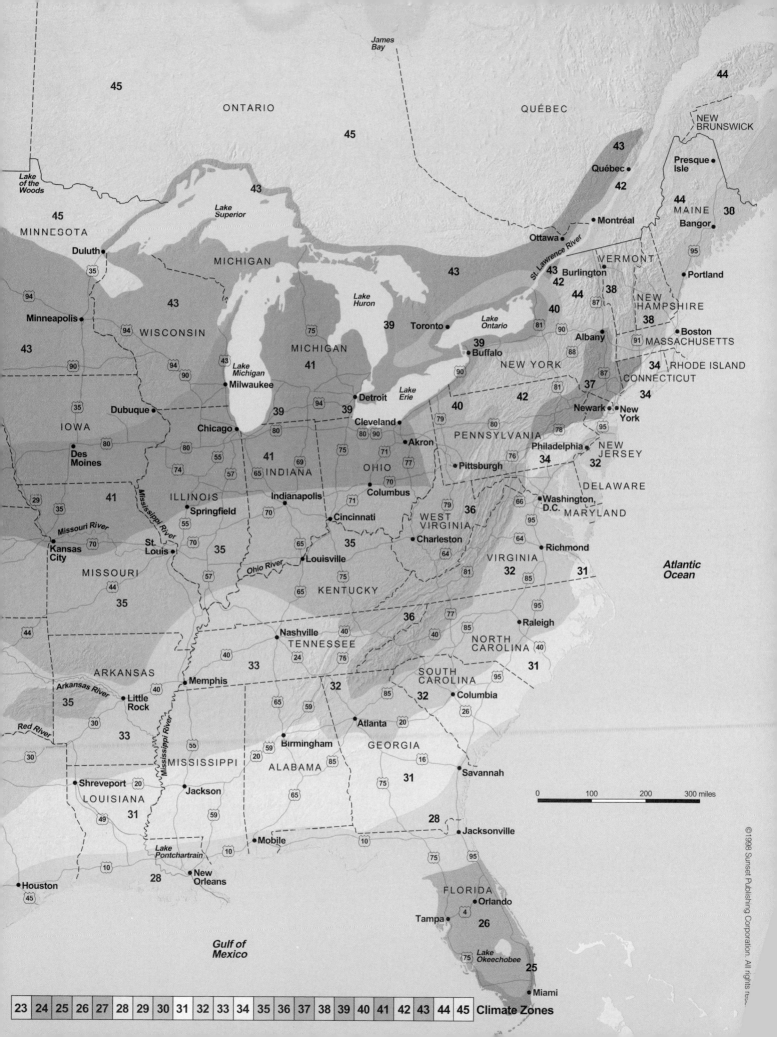

© 1998 Sunset Publishing Corporation. All rights res...

| 23 | 24 | 25 | 26 | 27 | 28 | 29 | 30 | 31 | 32 | 33 | 34 | 35 | 36 | 37 | 38 | 39 | 40 | 41 | 42 | 43 | 44 | 45 | Climate Zones |

INDEX

Page numbers in **boldface** *refer to photographs.*